DANCES
With
MARMOTS

DANCES
With
MARMOTS

A Pacific Crest Trail adventure

George G. Spearing

Magog Publishing, Oamaru, South Island, NZ.

To

Ziggy and The Gimp, Mountain Goat Vern

and all the characters and wildlife that took a part in the adventure.

Copyright © 2005 George Spearing

ISBN: 1-4116-5618-0

Magog Publishing, Oamaru, South Island, NZ.

Front cover designed by www.wolfcs.com

The Pacific Crest Trail

BRITISH
COLUMBIA
CANADA

Seattle
Olympia · Tacoma · **WASHINGTON**
· Spokane
Vancouver · Portland
Salem · · Snake
· Columbia
Grants Pass · Baker · Canyon
OREGON
Eureka · Mt. Shasta
Sacramento · **CALIFORNIA**
San Francisco
Fresno
Santa Barbara · Bakersfield · Mojave Desert
Los Angeles · San Bernardino
San Diego · Campo
MEXICO

— Snoqualmie Pass

— Timberline Lodge

— Ashland

— Sierra City

— Yosemite National Park (Tuolumne)

— Kennedy Meadows (Inyokern)

— Warner Springs

CONTENTS

California

Oregon

Washington

Epilogue

Chapter One

Inspiration, Uncle George, and the Mexican border.

I was going to hike the length of America.

It was Firefighter Kerry Hamilton's fault.

He'd been taking a break from the daily slog of rescuing damsels in distress, when he'd wandered up to me in the messroom of Auckland's Devonport Fire Station and handed me a book...

"Hey boss, wanna read this? You're into this kind of stuff."

Actually, the kind of stuff I was into at that particular moment, was a lump of springy gristle that should have been shot for impersonating a pie rather than to become one.

I reached for the book, running hot gravy up the inside of my uniform shirtsleeve.

Unknown to me, this uncomfortable instant in time was to be the, "starting gun" for a journey that would take me over thousands of kilometres, introducing me to a few more discomforts as well as some unexpected pleasures along the way.

The book was by Englishman Stephen Pern.

Ex-paratrooper and ex-everything else adventurous that you could think of, he had made a journey alone and off-road travelling entirely on foot through wilderness areas and national parks along the Continental Divide trail that stretched from Mexico to Canada.

The more I read, the more I realized just how predictable my life had become.

Here was a guy grabbing it with both hands and going for it...

He wasn't *reading* about it, he'd *done* it!

Stirring stuff!

I put the book down and wondered if I could do it.

Basically, for the past few years, the furthest I'd walked, was the odd stroll up to the corner store to get a carton of milk. With this in mind, I decided to leave my car at home one day and walk the twelve kilometres to work to see if I had the, "Right Stuff" for this type of adventure.

No problem!

I arrived at work smug in the knowledge that I'd managed to propel myself this vast distance without the aid of mechanical device or bus ticket.

There was however, a major flaw in this triumph - it hadn't occurred to me that the amazing feat had been accomplished on a pleasant summer's day, wearing light running shoes and shorts and with nothing more on my back than a T shirt and a warm breeze.

Part of the experience had also been to enjoy a pleasant stop at the Belmont shopping centre en route, visiting MacDonalds to buy a Coke, hamburger, and chips.

This was hardly Nanook of the North stuff.

Nor despite my imagination, even remotely comparable to, "Dangerous Dan McGraw" calling in at a desolate outpost to pick up beans and flour before heading out once more into the blizzard.

Ignorance was bliss though, and I'd blissfully convinced myself that there was nothing much at all to this walking business. Heading off Columbus-like in the direction of the Auckland City Library, I set about investigating a likely route through America.

After being awarded several parking tickets for abandoning my car whilst rummaging around inside for information, then sifting through stuff received from various United States agencies, I finally decided on a 4280km off-road route from Mexico to Canada known as the Pacific Crest Trail.

This trail was further west than the one that Pern had taken and to my mind had a few extra benefits.

One of its advantages was that the logistics of food supply would be easier.

Another was the fact that there was a publication available from an outfit called Wilderness Press that detailed the trail as well as providing all the relevant sections of topographic maps.

The cost of buying the complete set of topographic maps for the entire trek through America would have been astronomical - to someone contemplating becoming an unemployed itinerant, this publication was an excellent option.

The clincher for me however, was that my Uncle George lived near San José, which was at least in the same state as the first part of the trail.

The plan was to base myself there, practise looking like someone who knew what they were doing and then when I didn't look a *complete* wally, sort of ease myself nonchalantly and unobtrusively off into the unknown.

This trail was more remote and less travelled than its well known eastern counterpart the Appalachian and kept as far as possible from frequented areas. It stretched north from the Mexican border up through the desert areas of southern California, crossing the western end of the Mojave desert before climbing up into the Sierra Nevada range and then continuing on into the Cascade Ranges of Oregon and Washington.

It finally left the US in an area called the Pasayton Wilderness to enter Canada through the Okanogen Forest in British Colombia.

My B Grade Movie imagination had clunked into gear...I was the lean, steely-eyed, cowpoke/trapper/Indian fighter...the quintessential, "man alone" against the wilderness!

Blackie, my long suffering pet moggie, eyed me warily from the corner of the room. He'd grown used to my bursts of enthusiasm for various projects over the years, but he'd taken to giving me a wide berth on this latest one after I'd greeted him with, "Hasta la vista hombre!" and unsuccessfully attempted to lasso him with the video cord...Unless it involves food banditry, the mogster has no imagination.

I sat tall in my lounge chair, squinted into the sun and read on.

The route I'd chosen would take me through a mind-boggling range of terrain. From near sea level at the Columbia River on the Oregon/Washington border, to 4023m (13,200ft) at Forester Pass in the snowbound High Sierras. In total, 40 Wilderness areas, 24 National Forests, 7 National Parks and 3 State Parks would be traversed.

I would cross 19 major canyons, pass by up to 1000 lakes and climb 57 mountain passes - temperatures would range from very hot in the deserts of southern California to below freezing in the mountains of the Sierras and the Cascades.

Pull this one off George I thought, and you will definitely qualify for your, " Junior Outdoorsman Badge"

Reading on, it appeared that most people who hiked the trail seemed to only do bits of it, or else hiked sections over a period of years until they had completed the lot.

Figuring that the cost of the air fares was going to leave my bank balance teetering on the brink of death, returning too many times to do, "sections" just wasn't an option.

I owed it to my wallet to do the lot in one hit.

In any case, John Wayne wouldn't have done it in sections.

The problem with this though, was that the journey would have to be completed within a rigorous time frame of six months, starting somewhere near the beginning of April and ending around mid-October.

Leaving Mexico later than the end of April, would mean that the heat in the desert areas of southern California would pose dehydration problems.

If I left much before April, then snow and ice conditions further north in the high Sierras would still be extreme by the time I reached them.

On top of this, no matter what time I left the Mexican border, it was important to reach Canada before mid October when the snow began to fly in earnest, maybe forcing me to bail out, or get lost and end up a sad hairy popsicle.

With my route and timetable eventually sorted, I turned my attention to equipment and food.

It was obvious that a small but efficient range of clothing was going to be needed, along with basics of survival such as tent, sleeping bag, stove etc.

It also dawned on me, that as the only available transport was going to be me, then weight was a major consideration if I intended to actually move once I'd managed to pick all this stuff up and get it on my back.

Agonizing over all these details, it occurred to me that none of my western movie heroes had this hassle...they just slapped on a poncho, spat in the dust, and rode off into the sunset with nothing more than a canteen of water and a cheroot clenched in their teeth.

As it turned out my loaded pack, *sans* cheroots, averaged about 30kg (65lbs) and at one stage reached a totally depressing bone compressing 45kg. (100lbs)

As all my equipment began to pile up, it rapidly dawned on me why long distance hikers are a bit paranoid about weight. Some are even known to cut down the length of a toothbrush handle in their quest for lightness - Firefighter Finlay it was happily pointed out, had once even cut off the bristles.

This wasn't really fair, as Firefighter Finlay probably hadn't even done much in the way of hiking, let alone molested a toothbrush.

His only crime had been to be born Irish, and the firecrew, not particularly known for political correctness amongst themselves had leapt at the chance to create an, "Irish" joke.

Now, for an ex Belfast fireman such as Roy, who was no doubt used to dodging exploding shillelaghs, the small-arms fire from the crew's pathetic sniping was no problem at all and he had effortlessly put them in their place by throwing back a few jokes of his own.

He had then played his trump card by pointing out that it was an Irishman who had won a final heat in the television programme Mastermind.

This he advised them, was a show designed exclusively for *clever* buggers. "*Take that youse bastards!*"

Fire stations are not the place for sensitive souls!

I'd also discovered from my investigations, that some hikers on this trail had eaten over 6000 calories a day from their packs and still managed to lose weight.

So it was with some concern that I prowled around camping stores studying minute tinfoil packets half filled with lighter than air powder proudly proclaiming that they were a, "Hearty Meal For Two".

Who were they kidding!

I knew of at least two firefighters that could have eaten a carton load of them, then boiled up and eaten their canvas packs and still kept their heads in the trough!

What I needed was jam doughnuts and a Sunday roast, but civilian dehydration technology apparently hadn't cracked it yet.

With this in mind I contacted the NZ Army for advice.

I figured that these jokers operate in remote locations, carry huge weights around, and presumably still manage to eat enough to give them the strength to cause trouble.

"Try the Air Force", I was told.

I duly sent off a letter detailing my intentions and concerns, and respectfully requesting nutritional information.

I'm still waiting.

Maybe it's a secret.

I wrote away to the US and obtained an excellent two volume guide on the PC trail from Wilderness Press.

These included the necessary topographic maps for the entire route, excellent terrain description, and suggestions on where food supplies could be mailed awaiting pick-up.

Importantly, they also included the locations of reliable water sources - although on at least two occasions the reliable water turned out to be dust and sand. The publication had curled at the edges as an unhappy hiker hurled dehydrated curses at its blameless authors.

I was to develop a deep respect for fresh water and its critical importance.

I found out about an outfit based in Los Angeles called Trail Foods - this company would mail orders of dehydrated food to any postal agency for the date required.

They proved to be very reliable and my supply parcel would always be awaiting pick-up when I arrived salivating at one of the small and remote communities. These pick-up points were usually about 160km apart - the furthest being about 330km.

My method was to work out the distance between supply points, estimate covering 25km a day to see how many days food were needed, and then add one days food as a back-up.

I would have liked to have added a week's back-up and a couple of pizzas, but the extra weight would have slowed me up a week and made me burn more calories, so it was a catch 22 situation - a couple of sherpas would have been handy.

Having thus worked out my route and supply requirements but still not having done much in the way of hiking before, I disappeared with my pack into the Hunua Ranges south of Auckland for a three day, "dummy run".

This sowed a few worrisome seeds of apprehension into my plan, as I emerged at the end of it limping, with a sore knee and feet that felt like they'd been interrogated by the gestapo on one of their more pissed off days.

To compound my worries, there was a note pinned to my car advising me to contact the local police.

It turned out that someone had spotted my car sitting around for a few days, and had done their civic duty by notifying the constabulary. No problem, except for the knee and foot pain.

The problem with my feet was easily fixed by swapping my boots for a pair one and a half sizes bigger.

The knee was a bit more difficult however, but after peering at x-rays of the offending joint my doctor assured me that if I could put up with the pain, then nothing was going to suddenly go twang and leave me legless.

So, clutching a prescription for carton loads of anti-inflammatory painkillers, along with a cover note for customs officers explaining that I wasn't an international drug courier, I progressed to the next stage of the expedition, reminding myself that a bit of pain was to be welcomed as being thoroughly character building.

My next obstacle was getting the time off work, and also breaking the news of my pending absence to my girlfriend Sadie. I was a bit apprehensive about this, as most of the females that I have known, don't seem to hold Big Adventures in quite the same light as I do – it was a pleasant surprise though, to discover that she was quite impressed with the idea and offered no immediate resistance.

I was to discover later on though, that after she'd had time to think about it, she began muttering things about possible chance liaisons with Indian maidens, love-starved cowgirls and attractive mountain sheep. I found myself in the ludicrous position of having to convince her that most of my time would be spent miles from civilization and therefore temptation, and that there was no way I would have the inclination let alone the stupidity to hazard my important bits engaging in amorous liaisons with the wildlife of North America.

It ain't easy, this adventuring stuff!

Not wanting to completely sever the umbilical cord from Mother Fire Service, I decided to try stretching it a bit by applying for a years leave of absence. This was granted amidst great hilarity from fellow firefighters, who took pleasure in informing me that it was probably only granted on the odds that I'd fall down a ravine or get converted into bear turds.

So much for caring words of farewell!

I was duly presented with a huge, "going-away" card that had been drawn up by the daughter of one of the crew - it depicted a distressed cartoon of myself, loaded down and hobbling on crutches through a bear and reptile infested wilderness.

The stage was set!

All that was missing, was an increasingly nervous actor who didn't quite know his lines yet.

The BIG DAY finally arrived, and giving what I hoped looked like a devil-may-care slightly buccaneering sort of wave to Sadie and two of my crew who had come to see me off, I disappeared into the departure lounge of the Auckland airport.

I was a bit disappointed to realize that I was already beginning to hyperventilate and as yet there wasn't a bear or snake in sight - my most traumatic experience so far, was being robbed of $20 departure tax by an unsmiling airport official.

This first part of my journey was rather blurred. This was due partly to the free in-flight drinks and partly to the fact that my mind was a cartwheeling mass of information on places, dates, equipment and food requirements, all tangled up with nagging thoughts of self-doubt. Would I be able to hack it?

Would I get, lost/injured/mugged/murdered/eaten/exhausted/ beamed up by aliens?

Still, I guess that was what it was all about and there was only one way to find out.

The 'plane eventually touched down in Hawaii and I joined the long queue of disembarking passengers to approach my first US customs officer of the journey.

I'm always vaguely uneasy around the minions of bureaucracy, they stir up mild feelings of aggression in me - I think it's the no compromise, "I have the power" attitude of their ilk.

This guy seemed friendly enough though, but despite this, I approached him with the niggling knowledge that I'd pulled a bit of a swifty on his compatriots in the Auckland US embassy. One of the requirements at that time, was that any visitor to the States was required to prove that they had sufficient funds in their bank account to sustain them for the duration of their stay. I was requesting a reasonably lengthy stay and was a bit concerned that my account might not be up to the standard required by Uncle Sam.

I'd voiced my concern to Dave Quedley, one of the firefighters in my crew.

"No problem mate, I'll just biff ten grand into your account for a couple of days while you get your visa!"

He did that. I trotted along to the embassy with my new fat bank statement, impressed the man and got my visa.

I looked at the customs man. What if super American technology had accessed my bank status and exposed me for the near pauper that I was?

I put on my friendly face, "G'day!"

"What is the purpose of your visit?"

"I want to do a bit of hiking up through America."

"Where you goin'?"

"Off road from the Mexican border up to Canada."

10

(Did I say that?) I already felt like I was an imposter!

There was a long pause as he looked at me.

"So you're an Outdoorsman huh?", he said it as though I should have been wearing a coon skin cap and buckskins or something.

I shuffled in what I hoped was an outdoorsman-like manner and muttered, "Yep," hoping that I looked like Davy Crocket and sounded like John Wayne.

"Well I can't give you as much time as you're asking. You'll have to re-new your permit later on."

Fair enough I thought, grabbed my passport, and flew on to San Francisco where I disembarked and travelled by bus to nearby Mission San José. It was near here that my Uncle George lived in an isolated trailer home at the foot of the Diablo Range.

Uncle George was a bit of a hero of mine. He'd emigrated to the States from Scotland after his demob from the army in the forties. He was a grumpy feisty old bastard, his favourite adjective being, "goddam" and every object within sight was eventually labelled with it. He was a softy underneath it all though, and he meant a lot to me.

I spent a few weeks with Uncle George, sorting out details and testing my knee on the sunburnt range that stretched out beyond his home. The pain wouldn't go away, but at least it was bearable.

I borrowed Uncle George's pick-up and drove to the San Francisco immigration offices to attempt to get an extension on my permit.

It was hopeless.

The immigration waiting rooms were wall to wall with people from every corner of the Earth with a couple of other planets thrown in.

I waited four hours then gave up.

The only fun part of the day had been when I'd driven in to the city - I'd shot across an intersection and found myself heading the wrong way into a one way road system.

Luckily, on the corner to my right, was an abandoned service station. I hung a rapid right, got up over the kerb and was able to boot it into the

11

correct road.

Looking back to make sure that there were no agitated members of the SFPD in pursuit, I was amused to spot a car load of black Americans, stopped and facing the wrong way in the middle of the road. Looking totally bewildered as cars sped down either side of them. They had been behind me at the intersection and must have followed me across into the one way system. At least I wasn't the only one who made mistakes.

Sorry about that folks.

I returned to Uncle Georges' trailer home and tried getting through to immigration by 'phone, but they have this cunning system whereby it's impossible to actually speak to a living human.

You have to negotiate your way through countless recorded telephone instructions to find the department you want, and then grow old listening to recorded, "hold" music. One of the more frustrating aspects is that a recorded voice will ask you if you want the instructions in English or Spanish.

Twice I replied with, "English". Each time being immediately besieged with a torrent of recorded Spanish.

I thought about this. I was also getting cunning. The computer was obviously programmed to detect American accents.

I tried again.

"Do you want instructions in English or Spanish?"

Putting on my best John Wayne accent I drawled, "English, pilgrim."

Bingo! It worked, and I had the pleasure of following the instructions until hitting the, "hold" music.

I sat there with the 'phone clutched to my ear. My hair was beginning to fall out and I was sure I could detect the beginnings of age spots on the backs of my hands...Geese were beginning to fly south.

I finally gave up trying to speak to someone about an extension and sent them off a letter advising them of my problem and suggesting that if they wanted me, I'd be out in the woods somewhere heading for Canada.

I contacted the Trail Foods company in LA by 'phone, telling them of my plans to travel all the way down to the Mexican border by bus, changing buses at the terminus in downtown LA.
They advised against it.
The bus terminal in LA was too dangerous they reckoned. "You wander around on your own down there with a pack on your back and them bad guys is gonna think it's Christmas. Take my advice buddy and catch a 'plane all the way to San Diego."
They also told me that they were supplying an, "English guy" who was starting off a week before me and also heading for Canada.
I looked forward to maybe meeting up with him.

I had intended travelling by Greyhound bus all the way down to San Diego before catching local transport to the Mexican border. However, apart from the advice received from Trail Foods, the bus company was in the throes of a major drivers strike.
The company was using ring-in drivers, and the buses were being picketed and shot at - Welcome to the Wild West!
Deciding that one way or another travelling by bus might be injurious to my health, I flew down to San Diego. Uncle George had farewelled me from the porch of his trailer home with another bit of advice, "You watch out, this town's full of goddam crazies!"
I relished this, as he'd not long finished telling me about a couple of backpackers that he'd almost shot to death.
He'd woken up one night and heard some voices alongside his bedroom window. He opened the drawer at his bedside and pulled out his revolver. It was quite an ancient piece of artillery and had no safety catch.

"The goddam thing went off and blew a hole in the side of my goddam trailer."

The two backpackers, who were lost and had come down out of the hills to get their bearings, had dropped their packs and ran for their lives. A cop had turned up soon after daylight to retrieve the packs and find out what the story was.

Uncle George explained what had happened and told him that he needed the gun because there were, "So many goddam crazies prowling around here!"

He must have made an impression, because nothing further happened and the cop parted with the advice, "Just remember, if you ever shoot a prowler, make sure you drag him in across the doorway. That way there ain't gonna be a problem."

You don't mess around with Uncle George!

Unfortunately Uncle George is no longer with us.

But get this!

He died *standing up!*

"First one I've ever picked up like this", the undertaker had said.

They'd found him standing, stooped at his wash basin, and looking as though he was just about to splash water on his face.

He had not long before celebrated his 80th birthday, and my wife Berneece and I had been lucky enough to be there to get him a cake. Uncle George was different.

He'll be missed goddam it!

***

"Freakin' Marines!"

The expletive had come from the man behind the San Diego domestic air terminal information desk.

Apparently a young marine had asked if he could use the 'phone to call a local taxi, and had then spent half an hour talking to his girlfriend on the other coast - his drill sergeant would have been proud of him,

Initiative Training had paid off.

The harassed info man pointed me in the right direction for the bus to El Cajon, and I stepped out into the street and bright sunshine. It was only a short walk to the bus terminal and I watched with some professional interest as a San Diego Fire Department truck cruised by. I also noted that the crew were obviously appreciating the form of a young blonde girl that walked ahead of me. Ah, well, I thought, different Fire Department, same interests.

The small dusty bus terminal at El Cajon, about twenty five kilometres from San Diego, was my last stop before reaching Campo near the Mexican border and it was here that I saw my first Mexicans. Four of them stood grouped together looking rather lost and subdued. What struck me was their size. They were all quite small. Until then, my only experience of Mexicans had been Hollywood's grinning but deadly banditos. Maybe they got bigger and grinningly deadlier the further south you went.

A young policeman wandered in and made a beeline for them. They must have been there legally, for after several minutes of questioning them he lost interest and wandered off again. I mused at the fact that he hadn't even given this pack carrying alien a glance.

The lady at the ticket counter gave me the time of departure and asked where I was from. She'd once visited New Zealand, and handed me my ticket with some smiling advice, "You keep an eye on your pack now and don't walk away from it, this ain't Noo Zealand."

I watched the four Mexicans, and was relieved to see that they hadn't started grinning yet.

My bus was due to leave at 1509, and I watched as a small battered bus pulled in and then left again - I looked at my watch, it was 1455. 1509 arrived and there were no signs of any other buses.

I dragged my pack over to the ticket counter.

"When's the bus for Campo get here?"

"Just gone, it was that last one that left."

"When's the next one then?"

"Ain't but one a day. Next one is tomorrow."

Shit!

"I thought you said it left at 1509?"

She looked at her watch, "Well I guess they was a bit early. Don't always stick exactly to the timetable."

I was worried, the Mexicans had started grinning.

Just then another bus pulled in and the ticket lady spoke to the driver - the driver got on his CB and contacted my bus who waited for me a couple of miles down the road until I was dropped off by the second driver.

I was impressed by the service.

Couple of hours later and I was in Campo, about two and a half kilometres north of the Mexican border and about sixty five kilometres due east of Tijuana.

Campo had a population of around 1100, it consisted of a feed store, grocery store, post office and border patrol station.

Most of the inhabitants appeared to be employed by either the border patrol or sheriff's office, and as a Kiwi who was used to seeing the average policeman armed with not much more than a pair of handcuffs and a wet bus ticket, the amount of firepower they carried around was quite awesome.

I was relieved to find that the store could supply me with white spirits for my small stove and after inquiring where I could camp for the night, walked to the edge of the settlement and pitched my small one man tent for the first time.

A plaque on the wall of an old unoccupied stone building nearby, informed me that it was the scene of an attack by, "Border raiders" in 1875.

On Dec 4th, 1875, this attack had been the second largest, 'shootout' in the Old West's history.

The original store had been owned by the brothers, Lumas and Silas Gaskill. Both with a reputation as being hard, tough men.

Bandits, led by Pancho Lopez, had decided to raid them but they had underestimated the Gaskill brothers, and along with a couple of the locals who joined in the fray, the desperados were permanently removed from the scene after a furious and bloody gunfight.

Crawling into my tent, I hoped for a more peaceful stay.

I was to become an expert at pitching that tent, doing it almost every night for the next five months. To any question on where I was headed, my reply was, "North a bit." To say Canada seemed ridiculously ambitious at this stage - it was a bit mind boggling and I didn't want to think too much about the distance myself.

All the horror stories heard about travel in America filtered insidiously through my brain as I lay in my tent on that first night.

Sleep was fitful as I sub-consciously tuned in for the approaching sounds of Heat Seeking Rattlesnakes, Drug Crazed Vets, Grinning Mexican Banditos Out On A Border Raid, and Geographically Confused Texas Chainsaw Massacre'ists.

Thankfully, for the moment at least, psychotic bears, carnivorous cougars and sasquatch were off the list.

The next morning I picked up my food supplies from the post office and with the advice of, "Watch out for the rattlers, they comin' out now", I loaded up and began the two and a half kilometre hike south towards Mexico along a hot uneven sandy road. An open backed truck passed me as it bounced down the road, the half dozen dust covered workers in the back turning to stare impassively.

I felt kind of conspicuous as I staggered along under the unaccustomed load with my pristine untried gear and my pristine untried legs.

Canada? Strewth! Who was I trying to kid - and it was bloody HOT! Sweat ran down my neck in rivulets, soaking me within minutes of starting.

The pack straps were dragging on my shoulders and I was dehydrating under the jacket that I was wearing with the misconception that this would be the easiest way of carrying it.

I reminded myself that I'd just have to get used to it and miserably pondered the fact that there wasn't going to be an air-conditioned McDonalds waiting seductively over the hill this time.

I eventually arrived at my initial target - a rusting barbed wire border fence that shimmered into the distance across arid chaparral dotted land.

Just the word, "border" stirs something in me.

I may have read too many adventure books in my younger days, but for some reason I get a real buzz approaching and crossing borders and boundaries - Sigmund Freud work that one out.

Anyhow, here it was at last, The Biggie - The Mexican border!

The start of the Pacific Crest trail was marked by a lonely clump of carved wooden posts - that's good I thought, so far I wasn't lost.

I dumped my pack up against the marker and took a ceremonial photograph. Rather disturbingly nearby, nine unmarked wooden crosses about 5ft in height had been jammed down through the strands of the wire fence.

Later on, I was given two different versions for the reason that they were there.

One was that there's a fair bit of aggro along the border with drugs and illegal immigrants, and a cross was put up each time there was a death in the vicinity.

The other version was gleefully given, that a cross was put up every time there was a death along the trail.

Eight of the crosses were fairly weathered, although one looked rather unencouragingly like a recent addition.

18

Whatever the reason for their existence, these stark reminders of mortality, enhanced by their arid setting, did wonders for my imagination which was by now trampling on top of my brain to scan the horizon for any tell-tale dust clouds set up by the galloping horses of approaching Border Raiders.

Satisfied that the horizon was raiderless, I clambered through the rusting wires to stand on Mexican land.

My intrusion into Mexico was just long enough and far enough to be able to say that I'd been there, and I clambered back again to pick up my pack, take a deep breath and begin my trek north to Canada.

April 20th, 0920 hrs - I'd begun at last!

The Mexican Border

Chapter Two

Rattlers, Strange heartbeats, and Warner Springs.

My journey was to take two days short of five calendar months. At times I'd hike for a few days in the company of others I met along the way - Ziggy from Seattle, Tim, "The Gimp" from New Orleans and Vern, "Mountain Goat" Anderson from Michegan were good companions at different stages through California, though I hiked through the states of Oregon and Washington without company.
I saw less people on the trail than I had expected and the longest I went without sighting anyone was ten days. Even then, sightings were more often at a distance and went by without contact being made.

The sheer unspoilt vastness of America's wilderness areas were quite awesome, and provided a refreshing aspect to the US after a diet of American TV Big City cop shows and 'in your face' sitcoms.
People would later ask me if I ever got lonely.
The answer was, "No".

I may have been alone, but each day was completely filled with the goals of survival, taking in the environment and wildlife...and making sure I didn't step on anything that wriggled.
It's a rather sad comment I suppose, but it was a far lonelier experience wandering around crowded cities after my walk had finished.

With the exception of nine separate layover days, I hiked every single day for the five months, and over the entire period including the layover days, I was to average 28km a day.

My first target and supply point after leaving the border was Warner Springs. This small community beckoned like an island, 180km away through a sea of arid hills and the barren scrubby lands of the San

Felipe Valley, Anza Borrega desert and fringes of the Colorado Desert. The supply points I'd chosen were small settlements in areas where a road would intersect or approach the trail and on average they'd be about 160km apart. These distances were ideal for fooling my brain, as I could relate to that sort of mileage and knew that if need be, then these settlements were pull-out points. They also usually had a diner and as any long distance hiker will tell you, diners are the meccas of the foot slogger's world.

I knew that snakes and I would be neighbours for most of my pending journey, and not being of the same calibre as Steve Erwin the crocman from Oz, I looked forward to introducing myself to them with an interesting mix of enthusiasm and thinly veiled terror.

I had purchased a snake-bite kit especially for the occasion, and it was strategically housed within grabbing distance in my pack. The kit consisted of a sharp blade, two rubber suction cups of differing size and a string tourniquet. The theory was, that after being monstered by the snake, you opened up the bite wound with the sharp blade, located the appropriate sized suction cup over the wound, fit the tourniquet above the wound and then I suspected, lay down and waited to die from either shock or venom.

I had the feeling, that if I ever had to perform this First Aid on myself, I'd probably pass out at the first incision of the blade and bleed to death anyway.

I also spent quite some time pondering the question of where you would fit the tourniquet if you were bitten on the bum - the blurb that came with the kit didn't seem to cover that eventuality, which was a bit slack I thought.

Knowing my luck, if I ever got bitten it would probably be on such an uncool spot - "Yeah, poor guy got bitten by a rattler - had to amputate his butt."

My faith in the kit was further shaken, when I read an article expounding the theory that opening up the wound with a blade only helped spread the venom more quickly into your system - I didn't need this and wondered why the hell important advice on snakes, bears and the meaning of life, always contradicted itself.

None the less, I plodded along mentally practicing my snake-bite kit quickdraw, until I was probably the fastest in the west.

Faced down by Billy the Kid, I could probably have outdrawn and slapped a suction cup and tourniquet on him before he'd even cleared leather.

I'd never heard a rattlesnake before, and wondered if I would recognize the sound when I did eventually hear one. Let me assure you, when those critters rattle, you know immediately what they are!

I'd been travelling for about five hours through the scrubby rocky ground, when the attention getting spine tingling dry rattle stopped me in my tracks.

He'd spotted me first, and was reared up from the rocks in about four feet of don't-stuff-with-me attitude.

All previous ideas of cool snakeskin belt trophies and hat bands exited rapidly stage right along with their owner, as I put in some serious distance between me and an agitated serpent who wasn't interested in promoting apples.

Clint Eastwood would have stood his ground, eyed him down and blown him away with a lightning draw.

Yeah, good one Clint, but you didn't have a 60lb pack on your back and nothing but a Swiss army knife in your holster.

No doubt that old and innovative TV adventurer McGyver could have found a way of transforming the bit that gets stones out of horses hoofs into a Colt 45 - but I'm far less inventive, and concentrated mainly on preventing hyperventilation whilst setting a record for the 100 metre backpack sprint .

I'd read that rattlers can sense subtle changes in temperature and use this skill for detecting prey at night. They are also very sensitive to vibrations and can pick up footfalls at distances of over 15 metres away. Don't worry too much about it I'd been told, they'll likely hear you coming and slope off before you get there.

Wrong!

Either this one was vibrationally deaf, or he was feeling bored and thought, "Hey man, think I'll jus' hang around an' see how far this greenhorn dude can jump!"

One expert had told me that you can tell the age in years of a rattlesnake by the number of, "buttons" or segments on its rattle at the end of its tail.

This is probably true, but I never did get good enough at counting and jumping at the same time to be able to actually date one.

The snake slithered out of sight, and I carried on my way with an adrenalin boost equivalent to a fifty megaton caffeine hit, plus a new and intense interest in the ground around me.

I had the definite feeling that this journey was going to be a lot different to a wander around the Hunua Ranges spotting fantails.

Hauser canyon hove slowly into sight, and I made my first camp on the trail alongside a depressingly waterless Hauser creek. I'd been hoping to find water there as I was just about out, but it wasn't to be and I was lucky to squeeze just enough out of my bottle to reconstitute my tucker into a slightly moist powdery lump that peered unappetizingly up at me from the bottom of the pot. This wasn't too much of a problem though, as I knew that next morning after a 1000ft climb via Morena Butte I'd reach Morena County Park and some reliable water.

After a thirsty fitful night, the climb was made early in the morning before the sun pressed in and after filling my water bottles and myself I carried on to Boulder Oaks.

Genetically I'm half English, half Scottish.

Now that means that even though I enjoy a good adventure, half of me doesn't want to spend too much money doing it and any cost saving gives me a feeling that's almost as fuzzy as crossing borders. To this end, I was quite proud of my water bottles.

Most other hikers I was to come across had a variety of expensive and gimmicky containers that were either too heavy, too bulky, or too leaky. My containers were old 2 litre plastic soft drink bottles. They were practically weightless and could be flattened out to make more pack room when empty, and on top of that they were almost indestructible. (Fill one up and then jump up and down on it to see what I mean!) I say *almost* indestructible, because later on in the journey one succumbed to puncture by bear attack, but hey, who wouldn't?

Boulder Oaks held a camp ground and small store. It also has a road, so that meant easy vehicle access to the area. Because of this, I think it had become the favourite gathering place for the gun totting population of America - I climbed upwards towards the Laguna Mountains heading for Burnt Rancheria to the soundtrack of World War Three. Somewhere down below me some serious firepower was being demonstrated. Automatic gunfire was punctuated by the boom and crack of large calibre single shots.

I cast about uncomfortably, trying to locate their source and eternally grateful that at least I wasn't wearing my fur coat and Antler Hat.

Further on, tracking along the rim on the eastern side of the mountains, I could see a vehicle and several figures down in the distant valley.

The boom-crack of their shots reverberated along the valley below me. I couldn't see what they were firing at, but hoping that it wasn't me, I thought small and scurried along the trail making use of what cover there was until I was gratefully out of sight.

I figured that if I could see them, then if they looked up they were going to see me - and for all I knew they could have been the local branch of the Happy Psycho Club out on their annual picnic.

Burnt Rancheria was a pleasant camp spot with water, store, and shady pine trees.

In the later 1800's, cattlemen had moved in on the Laguna Mountains as the area was a good spot to fatten up their herds.

Unfortunately, the local Dieguenos Indians didn't think too much of the idea and demonstrated their displeasure by burning down a ranch house that the cattlemen had built. Hence the name Burnt Rancheria.

I dumped my pack and lay back in the shade of the pines, replacing a few calories and enjoying the local woodpecker percussion band. The volume put out by their assault on the tree trunks as they drilled for bugs was amazing. I'd never heard anything like it before. How they don't fall out of the sky with brain damage after spending all day methodically head-butting trees has got me beat.

It was here that I met up with two other long distance hikers heading for Canada.

Paul, "Ziggy" and Tim, "The Gimp" were two different personalities - a kind of Yin and Yang of the trail.

The bespectacled Paul from Seattle, was more of the thoughtful academic type, a BA studying for his MA. His skinny frame which got progressively skinnier as he headed north, belied his stamina and endurance and he, along with "The Gimp" made it all the way to Canada.

The exuberant Gimp was an, "In Your Face" Louisiana extrovert. If you wanted peace and contemplation you didn't walk with Tim!

But he had a crazy sense of humour that really appealed to me and I enjoyed the company of Ziggy and The Gimp on several days through California.

Ziggy had originally left the border in the company of a friend from Seattle. His intrepid friend had pulled out on only the second day, after getting a bit of a rev-up from one of the local rattlesnakes.

"Jeez! They got snakes an' stuff out here! See ya later dude I'm outta here!"

That amused me, as I thought that all Americans would be a bit blasé about their native fauna, after all, the kiwi doesn't bother me!

The Gimp had introduced himself at full smiling volume and stood there shimmering in the scrubby dusty heat of southern California, looking rather incongruous with snowshoes and ice axe strapped to his pack and clutching what I thought were two ski poles.

I eyed the snow equipment suspiciously and secretly got a bit worried - maybe he knew something I didn't know.

Surely it was too hot down here for snow and ice. Maybe the heat was a trick?

I had an ice axe and crampons, but they were still in the custody of Trail Foods, to be forwarded to me on request when I got a bit closer to the mountains.

We discussed our gear and I was relieved to find that he'd realized that he wasn't going to be needing the snow gear in southern California and that it was going to be a, "pain in the butt" lugging the items for hundreds of miles across snowless terrain. He mailed them away at the first opportunity.

"What's that guy carrying snow shoes for?"

"They ain't snow shoes, they're an old Inuit charm to keep snow away."

"But there ain't *never* no snow in these parts!"

"*See,* they work!"

Tim told me that he had got his nickname from his days on the Appalachian trail on the eastern coast.

He always hiked with a couple of poles he told me - which turned out to be things called leki sticks which are aids to support and have nothing to do with skiing or eastern block citizens, hence apparently his crippled or, "gimp-like" appearance.

Ziggy and The Gimp more or less teamed up and they tracked most of the way up to the Canadian border together

Having farewelled the duo, I left Burnt Ranchera and not too long afterwards coming down out of the Laguna Hills, learnt my first important lesson.

This particular stretch was reputedly very hot and waterless and I was reluctantly carrying just over 9 litres of water - the next chance of water was in Chariot canyon about 40kms away.

Nine litres of water weighs in at 9kg or 20 pounds, which is bloody heavy when you pile it on top of all the other crud you're carrying. (Why can't they find a way of dehydrating the stuff)

But ironically, and for the only time in my three months through California, it began raining heavily, accompanied by strong cold winds.

A tent loomed up out of the heavy rain, pitched right on the trail and I stopped briefly as its occupant called out.

The guy's name was Chuck, the atrocious weather had prompted him to stop in his tracks and get under cover.

Wise move.

It seemed ironic given the present weather conditions, but he'd run out of water and at his request I jettisoned a bottleful his way, glad to be relieved of the weight. I then made the mistake of pushing on to gain mileage and at about 1500hrs suddenly realized that bits of me were going numb and if I didn't get under cover quickly, then hypothermia was going to become another one of my new experiences.

I was fairly aware of the phenomena of hypothermia and knew that the recommended treatment was to administer warm drinks to the victim, strip him of wet clothing and then stuff him into a sleeping bag that was full of one but preferably two dry or naked members of the party to raise his body temperature.

This meant that if you were hiking with the Spice Girls, had a large sleeping bag and a crateful of warm lager, then it would be virtually *impossible* to die from hypothermia, even if you were endowed with only the *vaguest* interest in the meaning of life!

Unfortunately, this scenario was more than a gnat's whisker away from being impossible for the average bloke, and so regrettably I had to take steps to prevent myself from progressing to the treatment stage.

The immediate terrain was totally unsuitable for a campsite, but too bad, shelter was the priority and I dropped my pack, noting with alarm that the moment I stopped moving, the effects of the cold wind and rain increased. I couldn't get my hands or fingers to work!

Foolishly, I'd stowed my gloves deep inside my pack where they were doing a good job of keeping my spare underpants warm.

I kicked down some scrub on the rocky steeply sloping ground to make space for my tent and then using my teeth and hands as best I could, managed to get the tent up and dive inside.

My tent was too small to cook in without transforming myself into a fireball, so dinner that night was a few slices of cheese and some biscuits - not bad if you're a rodent, but not much of a reward for a 28km day with about 30kg on your back!

That early experience was a good lesson, and I never made the mistake again of pushing on for too long through adverse weather - or the mistake of stowing important gear where I couldn't immediately access it.

I can remember that day well, because as I lay there thawing out, I realized that my heart had started beating out of time - 4 beats miss, 6 beats miss, 10 beats miss, 2 beats miss!

Every time it missed, I could feel it jump in my chest. I'd never struck that before.

Strewth!

Maybe this was the build up to a main engine failure. It had me worried.

I'd been taking painkillers regularly for my knee since leaving the Mexican border and figured that maybe they were having a side affect on me.

I stopped taking them regularly from then on, but the problem more or less stuck with me for the remainder of my journey.

Depressing thoughts of a skeleton found in a mouldering tent accompanied my drift into sleep. In retrospect, the condition had probably been brought on by the unaccustomed stresses and pathetic diet that I was subjecting my body to.

The following morning I was pleased to discover that I was still a tangible part of the planet and that the weather was back to its usual temperate self, and progressing jauntily along to the rhumba rhythm in my ribcage I took in some panoramic views of the Vallecito Valley.

The valley was once the sight of a Butterfield Overland Mail Stage station that lasted from 1858 to 1861, the stagecoaches following an old Spanish trail from Fort Yuma.

Consulting my trail book, it informed me that the first Europeans to pass this way were Spanish forces led by a Lieutenant Pedro Fages, marching through this neck of the Colorado Desert in 1772 looking for deserters....I amused myself with ridiculous scenarios....

"Hey Pedro! Where you theenk we find deserters?"

"In a *desert* I theenk."

Descending into arid Chariot Canyon, I passed by several gold mines. Some abandoned, some apparently still in operation. It would have been a buzz to check out one of the mines, but the only two miners I met seemed a bit suspicious and not very hospitable.

My friendly greeting was met with silence and a sullen stare, so just in case I was being processed in their heads as an, "ornery claim jumper", I immediately moved on, exuding what I hoped looked like a total indifference to their boring old mine. They watched me closely until finally dropping from sight.

I eventually reached the small settlement of Banner. I'd actually deviated from the Crest trail to end up here but the sight of Chariot Canyon on my map, with its scattered goldmines marked by images of tiny crossed picks, had proved to be too much for me. Who could resist a canyon sprinkled with mines with names like Lucky Strike, Cold Beef, Golden Chariot, Golden Ella and Ready Relief?

I was Humphrey Bogart in Treasure Of The Sierra Madres!

After a brief stop to re-fill my water bottles at the small store I headed on for the San Felipe valley, overtaking another backpacker along the way. Eric was from Texas, and was doing some of the trail with his dog. What amused me was that they were *both* carrying backpacks.

"Hell yes", said Eric, "He can carry his own biscuits and water!"

The poor old mutt was looking a bit dishevelled in the heat, and Eric was concerned that the pads on his dogs feet were wearing off. It had never occurred to me that this could happen. I just sort of assumed that dogs were designed to wander around all day without shoes or socks on.

Apparently he was right though. Seems that they're only designed for short bursts and not the marathon, "walkies" that Eric had taken his pooch on.

His other worry was that every time his dog spotted a snake, the pooch would go ballistic and try and deal to it. As yet no fangs had found their mark, but Eric had a feeling that the odds might be running out for poor old Fido.

Their pace was a bit slower than mine, so I wished them well and headed on.

The mutt watched me dejectedly as I left, with a look that said he would much rather be checking out a lampost at the end of his street than hot-dogging it through the Californian scrub with a sack of crummy dog biscuits on his back.

The heat in the valley was totally oppressive and the following day I was glad to spot a lone dwelling with a log cabin built alongside it, a tree sprouting oddly from its roof.

Even better, the cabin turned out to be a bar, and prising my tongue off the roof of my mouth I staggered thankfully inside and dumped my pack against a wall.

An old timer sat alone in the cool darkness of the bar drinking a Michaelob beer from the bottle.

It turned out that he'd once stopped off in Auckland en route to the islands during WW2.

Seemed he'd been impressed by the physical size and pugilistic capabilities of the New Zealand Maori, which was not all that surprising really, as during his stay his nose had been re-arranged by one of them.

Anyhow, he obviously bore no grudge against Kiwis, for he shouted me a beer and opened another one for himself, punctuating the operation with a spectacular and resounding fart that by all the laws of physical science should have left his trousers flapping in smouldering shreds.

I was a stranger in a strange land, what should one do in such a situation?!

Did I politely ignore the explosion, or should I make some sort of comment?

A social quandary.

It was such a commendable example of pressure release that I decided on the latter.

"Jeez", I said, "I'm impressed!"

He looked up, "I ain't rude son, just damn fine beer!"

On October 6th, 1858, the first west bound stagecoach bounced up this valley on its way from Tipton Missouri to San Francisco - a journey that covered 4345km in under 24 days.

It ran for two and a half years, encouraged by the words of their boss John Butterfield, "Remember boys, nothing on God's earth must stop the US Mail!"

The equivalent distance was to take me five months, encouraged by the words of my Uncle George, "I give you two goddam weeks and you'll pack it in!"

Half a day away from Warner Springs I became tactically misplaced for the first time. *Tactically misplaced* was a soothing way of telling a pathetically insecure brain that I was lost, and the phrase was specifically designed to lull it into a false sense of security and stop me from panicking and running around in ever decreasing hysterical circles until I collapsed from dehydration.

I'd got smart and figured that according to my map, if I took off across the hills on a certain compass bearing I'd cut out a lot of messing around and short-cut to Warner Springs.

I can't really blame my compass or map nor claim that it was an unseen tidal current that took me off course, so I guess it was the dismal standard of my navigation. Anyhow, I ended up wondering just where the hell Warner Springs *was* exactly.

I eventually sighted a drilling rig a few miles off, so I swallowed my pride and headed for it.

The lone, "Hard Hat" at the rig looked at me as if I shouldn't have been let out on my own, spat a stream of tobacco juice into the dust and drawled, "You headed wrong. Warner's back thataways. You gotta cross over that ridge, lest you wanna cross Los Coyotes Reservation. Injuns shouldn't bother yuh."

Shouldn't bother me? - SHOULDN'T?!!!

Thwack! An arrow hit me right in the side of the imagination.

Okay men! Get those wagons in a circle - women and children in the middle!

(I'd spent my childhood wandering around in a Hopalong Cassidy cowboy outfit courtesy of my Uncle George, so I knew the drill.)

Hang on a minute George, there's only you, and your pack doesn't even have wheels!

Oh yeah, okay, plan B then - smile a lot and let the sun reflect off your bald spot. (Not much worth scalping there.)

As it happened, I wasn't bothered by, "Injuns" and finally bushwhacked down into Warner Springs in full possession of my remaining hair but hot and thirsty.

The first leg of my journey was over. My knee had held out and more importantly I found that my spirit was holding out.

I'd learnt to appreciate water, (ground temperatures in the San Felipe Valley had been right off my thermometer scale) become accustomed to the howling of coyotes every night, and met up with my first rattlesnakes.

The rattlers proved to be less of a problem than I had thought. Just as long as you were aware of where you were stepping or putting your hands (or other bits) they wouldn't bother you. In fact they are, as I've heard them described, the gentlemen of snakes, giving a fair old solo on the maracas to warn you of their presence. This was a big plus for someone coming from a country where there are no snakes and the most poisonous thing around is an uncommon spider that you have to practically stick your bits into its mouth before it'll bite you.

Having said that, there was one small catch.

There are a minority of rattlers that don't rattle at you before striking. This problem was increased by a 1960's rattlesnake elimination programme that eliminated the conspicuous noisy ones, leaving the silent ones to breed and increase their population!

I eventually met up with one such reticent character, who immediately slithered off in sulky silence. He seemed rather put out by the fact that he couldn't rattle and I felt a bit sorry for him.

Humming birds had been another new experience for me. I'd seen them on television documentaries of course, but to see them, "in the feather" as it were, left me with a feeling of wonderment. These minute flashes of colour looked more like a large colourful insect than a bird, and they struck me as the Harrier Jump Jets of the bird world.

I was intrigued by their aerial antics. They can hover, fly up, down, sideways and backwards, their little wings beating at around *70 beats a second!*

They're not slow on courage either and will see off much larger birds such as crows or hawks who invade their territory.

I'd also heard that they'd also have a go at humans as well, but none of the ones I met seemed to be very interested in me - perhaps I was considered a kindred spirit. I hadn't washed for a while, maybe I was starting to, "hum".

The biggest wildlife problem of the journey was to be bears, but as yet they were a thousand miles away.

I'd also by now discovered a new use for my false teeth. (Two teeth on a partial plate). I was carrying a walkman radio and found that lying in my tent at night, whenever I was able to pick up a station, the reception was improved by holding an aerial wire above my head.

This got a bit tiring on the arm but by hooking my false teeth through the mosquito netting above me, I could tie the aerial to these and lie back in comfort. - A smiling reception.

Warner Springs boasts a natural hot spring that was used for centuries by the Cahilla and Cupeno Indians. It has now become an attraction for tourists, though thankfully it didn't seem to be attracting too many while I was there.

The springs bubble up from deep below the surface, escaping along the Aguanga Fault which lies close to the small community.

The settlement took its name from John Warner, an adventurer who at 23 had initially ventured West on a trading expedition along with mountain man Jeddiah Smith. The six-foot-three Warner became known as 'Juan Largo' (tall John) by the Mexicans, and after becoming a naturalized Mexican citizen in 1844, had been granted 48,000 acres of land that contained the springs, whereupon he'd set up a ranch and trading post there. It must have been a fairly lucrative enterprise, as it was the only inhabited stopping place for wagon trains and stagecoaches between New Mexico and Los Angeles.

In 1846, thirty seven year old frontiersman Kit Carson had taken time out from Indian fighting, trapping and soldiering to take off his buckskins and enjoy a spa there.

Some time later in 1851, John Warner and two adopted indian boys held out against an attack on the ranch by a hundred Cahuilla Indians. They escaped with their lives, but the attackers stole all the livestock and set fire to the house and trading post.

This ruined Warner and he left the area never to return to his ranch.

This bit of history was interesting but at the time what interested me the most, was that Warner had a restaurant and a Post Office, and after eating my way through two breakfasts I picked up my supply parcel and squatted down outside the mail office to begin sorting out my pack.

It had taken me seven days of mainly hot thirsty walking to get here and it dawned on me that that was why communities were so insular before the advent of mechanized transport.

Hop in a car, hit a highway and I could cover the same distance in less than two hours with nothing more than the few callisthenics required to operate an accelerator and a brake!

Mr. Ford had made life easier, but I suspect that when he pulled up with his Model T in October 1908, he was towing a whole new trailer-load of unseen problems behind him.

The more I thought about this transport business, the more I realized that easy mobility has probably been responsible for helping to open up a whole new bag of social as well as environmental problems. Communities where everyone is known are rare and human nature being what it is, the anonymity made possible by rapid travel is ideal for performing a bit of mayhem.

Walking seven days to get somewhere tends to make you too knackered to cause trouble and too slow for a quick gettaway. I wouldn't like to be the only kid on the block without a car, but if no one else had one then I don't think it would bother me too much.

"Howdy"

My righteous contemplations on the evils of sensible and comfortable travel vanished and I looked up to see Chuck, whom I'd given the water to, collapse next to me in a sweating heap.

"G'day mate, see you made it okay."

I went on to tell him how I was royally pissed off at having lost a pack cover on the trail.

I'd fitted it over my pack during the downpour three days ago and was dismayed to find later that it had fallen off somewhere along the way. Oregon and Washington were bound to have a lot more rain and I would have been glad of it there.

He looked at me expressionlessly then dived into his pack, pulling out my pack cover that he'd found on the trail and wordlessly thrusting it towards me. Good on you Chuck!

Ziggy and The Gimp rolled in. For the next section, about 160kms, we'd hike on and off in each others company.

After eating, resting, eating and then eating before eating again, we moved out...slowly belching our way up into the hills and releasing various gases that had nothing to do with the Aguanga Fault. Chuck had stayed behind.

"Did ya see the way that motherfucker looked at me?"

The Gimp was referring to Chuck.

The Gimp had a way with words.

"I think I upset him or somethin'."

The Gimp could do that, to anyone who didn't know him, his full on exuberance could be an acquired taste. I think he'd struck a nerve when he'd made some derogatory comment on the state of Chuck's gear, which was mainly military surplus and dating from the American Civil

War.

The next few miles were spent inventing hilarious scenarios in which an upset and demented Chuck crept up on an unsuspecting camp to, "take out" The Gimp.

Chuck's plan had been to reach Canada, but I heard later that he'd pulled out not long after leaving Warner. I was sorry to hear that, I liked Chuck, he didn't say much, but he had found my pack cover.

The next stages would take me through more desert-like areas and into the beautiful mountains of the San Jacinto Wilderness and the San Gabriel range. The gnarled Limber pines near the summit of Baden Powell mountain are over 2000 years old and still alive - just.

It was something to stir the thoughts, knowing that I was sitting against a tree that was already sprouting when J.C. was a lad.

But before then, just after Warner, I came across a notable example of arboreal life that was hard to miss.

It was a conifer that produced *massive* cones. I picked one up and looked incredulously at it.

The thing had to be a genetic mutant - maybe its roots were tapping a radioactive subterranean stream. It occurred to me that I'd probably wandered into the Weird Zone That Nobody Talks About.

The US Government probably denies that this area even exists!

I furtively looked around for more mutants, maybe a giant spider or maybe even a sabre-toothed toad or two. Having satisfied myself that I wasn't about to be disemboweled by creatures from the Gamma Zone, I consulted my trail book. It looked like what I'd found must have been the species, "Big Cone Spruce". If it wasn't then it should have been, and if it was, then an even better name would have been, The Bloody Humungus Big Cone Spruce.

It wasn't a particularly large tree, but its cones were about the size of my head!

I'm not exactly a pin-head, having a fairly adequate sized cranium that complies with British Standard size seven, so I think I was justified in being impressed with their size.

It would have made an excellent conversation piece, "Oh that little thing? They actually grow the really big ones in Texas. They plant the tree then wait for the cones to fall off and strike oil, don't you know."….. As the old saying goes, "You wouldn't want one on the end of your nose for a wart."

Pine cones as big as yer 'ead.

Camped further north in Cascade Canyon – from where the
'Great Marmot Glove Heist' took place.

Chapter Three

Idyllwild, Big Bear City, Agua Dulce, Three Points and the Mojave desert.

Two days later ascending above the Chihuahua Valley. Head down, brain in neutral and beating up a hot scrubby trail dreaming of frosted cans of Speights, I came to a sudden halt as I spotted a small black snake.

It had a long cream stripe running down either side of its body and lay motionless in the dust at the side of the trail.

Maybe this lack of mobility was just a clever trick to get me within striking range.

I stamped my foot, it didn't move. I spoke to it, it didn't show the slightest interest. Hmm, I thought, it must have croaked. Here was my chance to examine a lifeless snake at close quarters.

I stood next to it and prior to picking it up gave it a last minute nudge with my boot.

Kazow! It took off like a Cruise missile.

If it hadn't been for the fact that my newly acquired irregular heartbeat had chosen that very second to miss a beat anyhow, it would have missed one then. I'd never imagined anything without legs could move that fast across the ground!

Thankfully it shot off horizontally and not vertically up my shorts, or my journey could have ended then and there from cardiac arrest.

I checked out some books at a later date and I think it was a Whipsnake or Striped Racer - well named I thought.

I continued on along the eastern slopes of Bucksnort mountain to camp for the night under a stand of Coulter pines on Combs Peak.

It wasn't the perfect campsite as there was no water around, but the panorama here was impressive and to the north where I was headed I could see the San Gorgonio Mountain and snowy San Jacinto Peak. A rocky spine descended southeast from the peak marking the Desert Divide and also making up part of the trail I was to follow. The Santa Rosa Mountains stood out above desert Coyote Canyon, whilst further to the east I could sight the vastness of the Salton Sea stretching out beyond the Anza-Borrego Desert State Park.

The Salton Sea is an 890 square km saline lake that was inadvertently created when diversion controls of the Colorado River burst through just below the California-Mexico border.

The resulting floodwaters filled a salt depression that has now become a lake with about the same salinity as sea water.

As I pondered over the incredible amount of water that must have flooded across the border, I immediately had visions of hundreds of illegal immigrants dressed in Bermuda shorts and sombreros, going for it as they surfed the big one into America.

The original, "Mexican Wave".

Joined later that evening by Ziggy and The Gimp, the following day unfolded in a haze of rocks, ribbonwood and chamise as we plodded on in the direction of Table Mountain's boulder-strewn southwestern flanks.

It was one of the hottest days we'd experienced yet, spurring an earnest search for water that we managed to get from a trickle of a creek near Tule Canyon. The water depth was too shallow to accommodate a filter, so we biffed some purification tablets into our bottles to keep the water honest.

Apart from the odd lapse, none of us took any chances with our drinking water. Before starting out on this odyssey, I'd thought that Giardia was what the Irish called their police force. It didn't take me long to find out that I had that wrong!

Giardia Lamblia the Trot Bug was loose in the US and even pristine looking water could be suspect.

The bug found its way into water sources via humans who weren't too concerned about transforming the landscape into an open latrine. From there it could be transported to seemingly safe and remote locations by birds and animals. The bug is totally debilitating and to become victim to it could have meant the end of a successful Canadian landfall.

This would have been disastrous and would have presented a classic case as they say, of the bottom falling out of my world on account of the world falling out of my bottom.

Disappointingly, on my eventual return to New Zealand I found that this insidious blight had become much more common there too.

Yet another crack in the, "Clean Green" image.

Thirst attended to, the tedium of the travel was eased by The Gimp's inventive running commentary on the fictional trials and fortunes of The Intrepid Three… "Episode Two, Ziggy Gets Bit." etc., etc.

The Gimp had also locked on to the fact that I was a keen advocate of Velcro tape (A Kiwi invention, that from memory is known as hook and loop tape in the US.).

Several items of my equipment ended up being either patched with it or incorporating it.

The Gimp would march along broadcasting mock commercials in his Louisiana accent, "George Spearing's Hook n' Groove Tape, Will hold *anything* (pause) Well *almost* anything, conditions apply."

We camped that night at the eastern end of Terwilliger Valley, coming down out of the mountains to cross highway 74 and enter the San Bernardino State Park, beginning an ascent into the San Jacinto Mountains.

Our highway crossing was rewarded with beautiful scenery and plant life that slowly began to change as we made our way north, providing an unusually attractive mixture of desert and high country life-forms, and climbing to 7000ft, we contoured down to Cedar Springs in our daily quest for water and to make camp for the night.

The weather had again turned unexpectedly cold, near freezing with strong winds and I was feeling tired and a bit irritable. Just as I was feeling all, "Gimped out" and wishing that the Gimp would, "sling his hook" and leave me on my own, he characteristically performed an act of generosity and shared some sachets of hot chocolate and marshmallows with us which was absolute luxury - I felt guilty about my unwarranted irritability towards the well-meaning Gimp, we'd covered 34kms that day and my feet were throbbing painfully, which probably didn't help as far as my demeanour was concerned.

Later on in the journey, the nerve endings in my feet would become completely de-sensitized, and I would be able to make your average firewalker look like a big girl's blouse.

I hadn't yet reached pedicurian nirvana, so in the meantime I lay there a disgruntled lump, unhappily throbbing and building character.

The following morning we decided to get smart and make a shortcut, thus cutting out a small loop of the trail.

I should have known better - the vast majority of shortcuts that I talk myself into usually end up becoming long-cuts.

Sure enough, this attempt was no exception and whilst we were generally headed in the right direction, we ended up burning more calories than need be as we bushwhacked our way along on compass bearing through slushy snow and heavy undergrowth. Eventually we intersected the comparatively easy-going trail again, having ended up cutting the distance in half but taking twice as long to do it. Bugger!

We were in high country now, beautiful but cold with large areas of snow. The stretch between Apache and Southwell Peaks was difficult, with snow already on the ground and when it started snowing again the trail became very hard to follow. It was to give a sobering example as to what parts of the Sierra Nevada yet to come would be like.

Climbing up through lodgepole pines, manzanitas and white pines, we passed by a turn-off that would have taken us up to Taquitz Peak. I mention this not because I particularly wanted to go climbing any more peaks than I had to, but as a point of interest.

The peak is named after a legendary Cahuilla Indian demon who reputedly lives thereabouts. Apparently he used to dine on unsuspecting Indian maidens and turn the weather nasty when the mood took him. Maybe Taquitz was having a bad day and that's why it was cold and snowing.

The good news was, that by no turn of the imagination did we look like unsuspecting Indian maidens - though as Ziggy pointed out and I had to agree, a couple wouldn't have gone amiss.

Just before we could get ourselves lost again, we made it to the head of the Devil's Slide Trail that led down into the mountain resort community of Idyllwild. We held a quick conference and decided to make camp up in the snow before descending the next morning.

It was bitterly cold when we stopped moving and we rapidly erected our tents and disappeared inside, alone with our thoughts for the night and a bit apprehensive of the pending High Sierras after this taste of snow.

This pattern of camping above a settlement before entering it in the morning was to become a habit of mine for the remainder of the trip. Even if I got above a town in mid afternoon, I would tend to wait out until morning.

The reason was simple - FOOD!

I'd become addicted to heavy duty, gut expanding All American breakfasts! Many of the diners had separate menus for different times of the day, and I wasn't taking any chances - I wanted the Breakfast Menu!

Several lean days were spent drooling over the thought of plates stacked with pancakes, bacon, eggs, toast and hash browns drowning in maple syrup and washed down with high octane coffee.

Jenny Craig eat your heart out!

I wasn't alone in this obsession with food. For many of the male distance hikers I spoke to, their journeys were the first times in their lives since being breast fed that they'd thought more about food than, "the other".

Interesting how nature prioritizes.

We set out for the town below first thing in the morning, once more dropping down past the snowline and into more inviting temperatures. Right on the town edge, nestled in the trees and one of the first buildings we came to, was a diner.

A large sign above it proclaiming that it was named the, "Cheff In The Woods".

The ever alert Gimp spotted it, "Hey man! Lookit! This is where the goddam CHIEF of the woods lives!"

We piled in and started eating.

I'd just finished my second breakfast and was ordering some more toast.

The waitress paused from writing in her order book and looked down at me, "Y'know what? In a few more hours we'll be starting our lunch menu, and you'll be able to keep right on going!"

The day was spent sorting out supplies and getting some mail away. There was even a letter of encouragement from Blair Irwin, a hiker from San Diego whom I'd met further south. He'd been doing sections of the Pacific Crest Trail over a period of ten years, hoping to eventually complete it all one day.

I'd also called into a ranger station, hoping to find a ranger who could identify a snake that I'd seen previously on the trail. I'd felt sure that they would be familiar with just about all the wildlife in their area and had expected an unhesitating response, something like, "Yep! What you saw there buddy, was a non-poisonous female triple banded fang leaper."

I was disappointed to discover that they didn't have a clue.

Previous to this trip, I'd kind of imagined that rangers did a lot of just that, ranging. I was to find out that they didn't seem to do much of it at all. In fact, in the five months I walked I only ever saw one further than a roadhead campground, and that wasn't too far. In fairness, they're probably just too thin on the ground to be able to leave the main policing areas.

We pitched our tents in the well facilitated campground - $2 for distance hikers, $10 for others - a nice touch.

We'd enjoyed a good shower, re-stowed our packs with the new supplies and turned our thoughts to the evening.

The evening of course, was spent in a bar. Pizzas and beer.

The pizza was a mistake.

"Pizza with Jalapenos, you gotta try it man", beamed The Gimp.

"What's Jalapenos?"

"They're a real hot chilly", advised Ziggy shaking his head, "you'd better be careful."

I considered this, but decided what the hell, I could eat curries that would cauterize a severed leg.

Minutes later I felt like I'd been brushing my teeth with a flame thrower.

Jeez they were HOT!

I forced myself to eat as much as I possibly could, to prove that I wasn't a total wimp and to preserve the honour of all Kiwis. Then with studied nonchalance, doused my steaming head in a bucket of beer.

I'd hoped that my discomfort wasn't too obvious, but there was no fooling Ziggy, who sat there grinning as he studied my bulging eyeballs and wisps of steam that were emanating from my ears, "Told yuh, yuh wouldn't like 'em!'"

0500hrs the next morning I propelled myself out of my tent like an off-course space shuttle heading for an emergency landing in the campground latrine.

Jalapenos are a mistake of nature - they even burn you when they leave you.

We climbed back up into the San Jacintos, temporarily forsaking the Pacific Crest trail to make our way along the Marion Ridge trail that met up with the PC trail a little further north.

Pushing up through the pines, rocks and snow, we spotted a horseman, pack horse in tow picking his way slowly down towards us. He surely looked the part. Straight out of the old west - well worn gear, stetson, chaps, saddle bags, rifle, beard.

I was impressed, I watched as he drew closer, I bet his name is Shane or Cheyanne or Missouri or something!

His name was Fred.

Fred was doing as much of the trail as the terrain would allow. He was a real genial character and his appearance and mode of travel took me straight back to the Saturday morning cowboy movies of my childhood. We wished each other well and he continued on down towards Idylwild.

Unfortunately, I later learnt through the bush telegraph that he had abandoned his journey after one of his horses had taken a bad fall on roughly sloping ground. It had broken its leg and he had to shoot it. Sad moment, I felt for him.

We were about twelve kilometres north of Idylwild and heading for Fuller Ridge when we passed Johnnie.

Johnnie was lean and wiry and hunkered down collecting some water from the snow melt, his pack propped up alongside. So what? Well, Johnnie was 75 years old.

Here he was alone, way up in the mountains and heading for Canada he assured us. His attitude was helium for the spirit!

We introduced ourselves, and on hearing my voice he squinted up at me,

"Foreigner ain't yuh."

It was more a statement than a question.

Ziggy, The Gimp and I looked at each other, then burst out laughing.

I guess I was. Funny that, I thought that *they* were all foreigners!

From then on it became the buzz-sentence whenever we met up,

"G'day Gimp, Ziggy."

"Hi George, foreigner ain't yuh."

Johnnie's knee was giving him problems, and he spotted the thong-like knee strap that I was wearing to alleviate my on-going knee pain. The strap that I had brought with me from NZ was actually made in the US. It seemed to be working for me, and at his request I gave him the address of the manufacturer.

We left him slowly picking his way along, one slow step at a time. There was no way he would make it to Canada before winter set in. He had a dream though. Good on him.

Due to snow, we lost the trail a short time later and again reverted to heading on compass bearings. Some steep traverses of icy snow were made and my ice axe, still at the moment in the care of Trail Foods, would have come in handy. I don't know how Johnnie fared on this stretch, a fall could have been quite serious. We toyed with the idea of waiting for him, but eventually decided to carry on. We all had a long way to go, and none of it was going to be easy. At least he would have had our footprints as a lead.

A few hours later we located the trail and camped for the night on Fuller Ridge, a rocky fir-covered spine stretching away into the northwest and separating the San Gorgonio and San Jacinto river drainages.

We left early the next morning and eventually began the long hot gruelling descent down into the Lower Sonoran Colorado desert.

My left shin felt as though someone was twisting a knife into it with every step I took.

Maybe this was shin splints. Whatever it was, I was worried.

Ziggy and The Gimp, appreciating that this could mean the end of my ambitions, gave me the look normally reserved for someone who's just been told that they've got a terminal illness and carried on ahead, soon disappearing from sight.

My progress was just too slow for me to keep the pace and I was reduced to shuffling along with slow painful six inch steps, gradually closing the gap between me and the small community of Snow Creek.

I eventually limped into the small and seemingly deserted settlement and looking for water, knocked on the door of the nearest house. There was no answer so I filled my water bottles from their outside tap, erected my tent in the desert and crashed out in my sleeping bag, thankful to at last get the weight off my legs.

This was bad news, if my shin was giving me the same pain tomorrow, I would have to accept the fact that it looked like my body just wasn't holding up and seriously consider terminating my journey. I silently praised the foresight of my doctor back in Auckland and got stuck into the anti-inflammatory/painkillers again before drifting off to sleep, desperately willing myself to heal.

I awoke early the next morning and lay there for several minutes, not daring to test my leg. I eventually took the plunge and gave it a bit of a wriggle - it didn't feel sore. I got up and gave a tentative hop - perfect! I couldn't believe it after the intense pain of the day before! I was light-headed with relief…Spearing rides again!

I took off down across the Coachella Valley with the steps of a pardoned man, and having crossed the sandy wind-blown and waterless Gorgonio River, passed under the bridge that carried Interstate 10 to emerge onto more dusty arid land.

I was beating about on the edge of the hot scrubby desert trying to decide which direction I should head in, when I saw a man approaching me. He'd evidently come from a lone house that I saw in the distance and I turned towards him.

"G'day"

"Hi there. Where you headed?"

"Canada, along the Crest trail."

The man's name was Don Middleton, and he invited me over to his house to meet his wife Helen and take a drink. They were a real friendly couple who had forsaken life in the city for one that they liked in the desert. We sat in their back yard drinking iced lemonade. An incongruous small patch of grass that Don had nurtured from seed stood out in startling green against the dusty fawns, browns and greys of the surrounding dry terrain. Don showed me some of the artifacts that they'd come across in the desert, amongst them an ancient rusting spur.

Vibrations from the past.

"We appreciate what you're trying to do, and we admire your determination. Hope you make it."

I farewelled Don and Helen and added them to my list of thank you cards that were eventually dispatched from Canada.

I began the long hot climb towards the San Giorgino Hills. Trekking past the mouth of Cottonwood Canyon and into Gold Canyon, passing by the Mesa wind farm with its large propeller-like windmills generating electricity, and continuing onwards before making camp a couple of days later just south of Holcomb Valley and the site of the old gold mining camp of Belleville.

Looking back at my journal, I see that my comments for this part of the trek include, "Every part of my body seems to be aching, each part taking its turn to hurt the most."

One of the quirks of my journey, was that I often came to almost welcome a new pain.

The reason for this was that it took my mind off the part of me that was *currently* hurting.

It crossed my mind that I could have been on to something here, maybe with a bit of PR work I could run guided tours for masochists…"Blisters and pain guaranteed - De-luxe excursion includes a dose of giardia, a snakebite and a poke in the eye with a cactus.

Money-back refusal if dissatisfied - Insults extra."

This part of California had a rip-roaring history.

Holcomb Valley was named after a William F. Holcomb who had once prospected in the mines of the Sierra Nevada's Mother Lode, but besides that he must have been something of a crack shot, for he had been hired here by other prospectors for his ability with a rifle.

He'd been trailing a wounded grizzly when he came across signs of gold. This was in the 1860's, and soon after the word got out, every man and his dog turned up. The camp of Belleville sprung up, turning out to be one of the most lawless of the Californian gold camps. Which isn't that surprising when you realize that a census taken in California around about then showed that the average age of the population was in the twenties, there was only *one* female to every *thirty* males and the normal restrictions of law, family and home was non-existent for most - dangerous combinations.

Arguments and fist fights were frequent and usually broke out over claim jumping, thefts, and whose side were you on in the Civil War. There were a load of Southern sympathizers in the camp, as many had been kicked out of the pro-northern camps in the Mother Lode. Over forty men eventually died from hangings or gun battles.

I thought about this and decided that if the rebel Gimp had turned up here some years earlier, then on one side or the other, there would surely have been at least one more added to the toll.

I hoped that they all rested in peace - I was too tired and sore for any scary visitations from restless spirits.

I broke camp just after daybreak and arrived above my next supply point of Big Bear City early that afternoon.

After once more meeting up with Ziggy and The Gimp in the Van Dusen canyon, (Hi George! Foreigner ain't yuh.) we descended in bright sunshine to the small town.

Big Bear was a kaleidoscope of luxuries!

Restaurants, stores, laundromat, bars, motels and a Post Office.

The inhabitants seemed friendly and interested in what we were doing. One man gave us a lift to the Post Office to pick up our supplies, entertaining us along the way with a passable imitation of a Dr. Doolittle English accent. Another gave us a lift to the local park, "Just see the guys working there. It ain't a campground but they'll prob'ly let you guys put up your tents for the night."

They did, and Joe, Conrad and Andy opened up a storage shed and let us stow our packs for the duration of our stay. Unfortunately, we didn't manage to get much sleep on account of some mutt that kept up a continuous bark all night. It didn't even pause for breath. I think the damn thing had perfected a technique of breathing through its backside.

If I'd got hold of the thing, I would have ruined its skills forever with the insertion of a size 9 boot.

After conferring, and having been lulled into a state of decadence by all the surrounding amenities, we decided to spend an extra night in Big Bear. We also resorted to the ultimate decadence and spent it in a motel! (Motel 6, We'll keep the light on for yuh!)

I awoke the next morning and lay there luxuriating in the fact that I didn't have to get up, cook breakfast, pack a tent and start walking. The feeling took me back several eons to when I was a young lad in the throes of naval training - every morning began at some ungodly hour when we'd be yelled out of the hut to stagger off on an early morning run before the last notes of reveille had faded into the mist. Whenever I got home leave, for the first couple of mornings I'd set my alarm for reveille time, just so I could wake up and savour the experience of not having to double out into a cold dark morning!

I was sitting outside the mail office, sticking stamps on some postcards, when a large blonde woman in her thirties approached. "Ver are you from?"

I just managed to tell her before she informed me that she was from Germany and then let loose with a blistering tirade against Big Bear and its entire population.

"Zis iss not a good place to stay. I haff lived here for two years. Ze people, you think zey are friendly - Ha! It is all phoney! Zey do not care for anyone but zemselves!"

The Teutonic maiden was turning crimson. I looked around uncomfortably, the place was quite crowded and heads were beginning to turn.

"Thanks, I'll remember that, sorry, got to go now." I beat a hasty crab-like retreat.

She called out after me, *"It iss better you leave ziss stinking place!"*

She was probably just having a bad *herr* day.

I was beginning to wonder though, earlier on I'd passed a dishevelled and wild-eyed looking individual as I came out of a store. He'd come straight up to me and muttered, "I ain't takin' no messin'... I done time in San Quentin...I'll get me a gun and show them suckers." I politely agreed with him and beat another hasty retreat.

Maybe I attracted these sort of people. Maybe I needed a shave or something.

After an abortive attempt to get a meal at one diner on account of the spaced out lady owner appearing to have drunk a little too much to be able to remember our orders, we considered The Gimps' observation that, "The next time she comes outta that goddam kitchen she'll prob'ly be swingin' a freakin' axe or somethin' " and decided to retire to the nearby Blue Ox restaurant and bar.

The Blue Ox was neat. You waded across a sea of discarded peanut shells to get to a seat.

Free bowls of peanuts were everywhere, with signs, "Please throw your empty shells on the floor."

ALL RIGHT!! My kind of restaurant!

It was here that I was reminded that American English can have some subtle differences.

I'd struck up a conversation in the bar. The guy was taking some time out in the woods to get his act together. Lamenting the fact that his girlfriend had just recently shot through on him, he'd given me the story, then added, "Then she up and tells me that she's leaving me...man I was pissed!"

Now, when he told me he was pissed, I assumed that he either meant,

a) His girlfriend had left him because he was drunk. Or,

b) After receiving the news of her imminent departure he had proceeded to get legless.

Wrong! By pissed, he had meant that he was really annoyed!

Now, if he had added the word, "off", as in "pissed off", I would have understood entirely what he had meant.

But they don't. A subtle and confusing difference.

Accents too could take a bit of getting used to. My first experience of this was not long after my arrival at Uncle George's.

I'd sat down in his local diner and was attended to by the waitress, order book at the ready. "Super Salad?"

"Hmm", I thought, that sounds good. Must be some sort of super sized American salad.

"Yes please", I smiled.

She looked at me a little strangely and repeated her question, "Super Salad?"

I sensed that something was going wrong here, but couldn't figure out quite what it was.

"Yes, I'll have one of those thanks."

The hand holding the order book came down to her hip and she looked irritated.

"Do you want SOUP or SALAD?!!"

I meekly ordered the salad and she unsmilingly took off to no doubt tell her cohorts about the congenital idiot at table three.

Whilst on the subject of diners, *never* order a cup of tea. You're likely to get a lukewarm cup of water, with a wrapped teabag stuck in the saucer alongside. Stick with coffee.

They can't do tea.

I think it must be something to do with a party they once had in Boston.

I took time here to give Trail Foods in LA a call and sort out a minor hiccup in the ordering system. As I still hadn't seen or heard anything of the, "English guy" that they had told me was also walking the trail and heading for Canada, I took the opportunity to ask them of his whereabouts.

"Oh that guy quit at Warner Springs. Reckoned the trail wasn't what he expected it to be."

This intrigued me. Just what had he been expecting?

As far as I was concerned, the trail had already provided for a whole gamut of expectations - heat, cold, snakes, scenery, coyotes, colourful characters, hunger, thirst, pain and bliss!

What more was there to expect?

Maybe he hadn't expected *so much*. His loss, he should've hung in there.

We set off once more with stories of the Mojave desert ringing in our ears.

"You gonna need plenty of water there."

As it turned out, the Mojave was probably one of the easiest places to get water. Anyhow, that was over 320kms away as yet.

My main concern at that moment was the weight of my pack. One of the downsides to re-supplying was that you had just got your load down to something that wouldn't rupture the average pack horse, when whammo, it was Weight City again. One consolation was the hot spring that I knew was waiting towards the end of the next day.

After two days of hot travel through the usual array of herbage, Ponderosa and Jeffrey pines, sagebrush, chamise and chaparral, we reached the natural hot springs of Deep Creek.

This really was luxury for a weary body. The bubbling hot waters were surrounded by high rocks, grass, trees and hills. I got all my gear off and dissolved away the trail dirt.

Ziggy and The Gimp were a bit more demure, and took the plunge modestly wearing their shorts - I figured being a Foreigner had to have some perks, and a bit of exposure might as well be one of them.

The spot was a welcome stop but somehow had an unsettling feel to it, almost as if someone or something was watching you. I was intrigued later on to meet up with another hiker on the trail who without any prompting from me, commented that she felt there was something eerie about the place and was glad to leave it.

She'd been there some days before I began leaping around *au natural* - so it wasn't my fault.

Our day ended several pounds lighter from the grime that we'd washed off, and we camped at an arched bridge spanning the creek.

Our continuance north took us past Mojave Forks Dam, then on to Silverwood Lake to make camp at a windy and rapidly cooling picnic area.

A Canadian hiker approached us. Like The Gimp he'd done the Appellation trail in the east. I think he'd contracted a virulent form of verbal diarrhoea. It was obviously nearing the terminal stage, but I was too tired to minister to him. The Gimp closed in on him, and they were soon locked in verbal combat.

I caught Ziggy's eye, raised my eyes to the heavens and retreated out of earshot to contemplate my navel and the sounds of silence as I cooked up my evening dehydrated delight.

We eventually reached Cajon Pass and a six lane Interstate and railroad via Little Horsethief and Crowder Canyons.

The Pass has the privilege of being situated on the San Andreas Fault, which if you are going to find a fault with something, then this is quite a major one - Ask the citizens of San Francisco.

A lonesome looking memorial reminded us that the Santa Fe Trail pioneers had passed by here, while at the same time our stomachs reminded us that we were bloody hungry.

We had food in our packs of course, but any chance at *real* food was always seized at with the grasp of a shipwrecked mariner.

There was a road here, a road means people, and people meant food. A desperate scan up and down the highway revealed what looked to be a diner about half a mile away. We were now capable of detecting diners at 5 kilometres by smell alone.

We were not wrong, and entered Tiffany's 24 hour cafe, three desperate men. The place was full of the usual truckers and road traffic, and gracing the walls were at least three pictures of John Wayne.

I thought of my brother Ken now living in suburban Basildon, England. He was a big fan of The Duke.

He would have loved it here.

I've heard that the, "Golden Arches" have marched even as far as this spot now, and I'm picking that the portraits of Big John have now been replaced by gaudy pictures of Ronald MacDonald.

Sad.

As Ronald would say, "That's progress, pilgrim...d'you want fries with that?"

Full of steak, eggs and coffee and climbing once more into the hills, we looked back down at the Pass. A freight train that must have been

58

almost a mile long wound its way slowly out of sight. Trains always give me the urge to travel, which is just as well as I had a long way to go.

Two days later, after climbing into the San Gabriels, we descended down Sheep Creek truck road to reach the access road into Wrightwood.

Approaching the town, I looked up to sight an advertising billboard.

"DICK WILLARD FOR SHERIFF", the billboard had originally proclaimed.

However some local wag had been at work with a spray can, and had painted "BIG" in front of the Dick.

That billboard still gives me a chuckle.

As Mae West would have said, "Howdy sheriff, is that a gun in your pocket, or are you just pleased to see me?"

We'd only been in town an hour, and already we'd had two kind offers of accommodation. We ended up accepting the generous offer of Francis and Ursula Ferrance. Francis was an English teacher, and he commuted to his university daily. They told us that it wasn't uncommon for people to commute from here to San Bernardino and even Los Angeles to get to work. Must make for a long day.

Their children were away, so we had the privilege of using the comforts of their beds. Ursula even provided us with a slap up breakfast the following morning. The kindness of some Americans was to impress me many times on this journey. I'd left for the States quite prepared to dislike its inhabitants, but most of the ones I met wiped out any chance of that. No doubt I was frequenting areas that attracted and bred a different type of citizen to their Big City cousins, but I guess that's pretty universal. There was a certain, "vitality" to America.

After reaching Canada, I had a conversation with a Canadian that maybe goes some way to explaining it.

He'd asked me what my impression of Americans had been. "I found most of them very friendly and outgoing", I'd replied.

"You're right", he said. "You know what the difference between a Canadian and an American is?"

I was curious.

"Well, a Canadian will be standing on the corner and a big shiny late model BMW will drive by. He'll look enviously on as it passes, and then complain and moan because he hasn't got one. The American on the other hand, is optimistic. He will look enviously as it passes by and and say, "Man! What a car! I'm gonna get me one!" And he will. He'll either work 'til he gets one, or he'll steal it - but he will get one! It's because we're a Welfare State. We're too used to handouts. It finally rots you."

I'd previously told him that I found Canada and its people to be much like New Zealand apart from the accents. Maybe there was something in his theory...but maybe I'm just being pessimistic.

Ziggy's sister Allison turned up in town to rendezvous with the Zigster and get some more food into him before he turned transparent. Luckily for The Gimp and I, Ziggy's father had also given her some extra money with which to shout any companions he may have had with him.

Allison treated the three of us to a solid meal in one of the restaurants. Like I said, the kindness of some Americans!

Ziggy and The Gimp left town early next morning, but I stayed on until mid-afternoon, attending to mail, food, etc., and putting off the steep climb along the Acorn Canyon trail that led out of Wrightwood. I wanted some time out on my own anyhow.

My next supply point was to be Agua Dulce, about 148kms away but there wasn't much mileage made that day. As usual, civilization had eroded some of my hiking power and I made camp in the Angeles National Forest at deserted Guffy campground, an unimpressive six kilometres or so out of town.

I hadn't taken on a full load of water from Wrightwood as there was supposedly a good water source just down from my camp in Flume

Canyon.

There wasn't. The spring was just about non-existent with hardly enough water to wet your tongue. Maybe there had been some sort of shift in the ground, because there certainly wasn't much water reaching the surface now. No panic though, I would be a bit dry that night and my rehydrated meal was rather more crunchy than usual, but I knew that a ten kilometre hike would get me to water the following day.

It took me five more days to reach Agua Dulce. The arduous ascents and descents of Baden Powell and Williamson Mountains started off a stabbing pain in both my shins and I was popping my painkillers regularly now. I don't like taking medication of any sort but without them I wouldn't have liked to have thought of the outcome.

The heavy pack weight and continuous daily pounding that my legs were taking was having an affect. The painkillers were all well and good but I realized that by masking the pain, which was my body's way of telling me to try lying down for a week, I could be doing some irreparable damage. I could see no alternative though, I'd invested too much in this trip, both emotionally and financially to consider pulling out unless I *really* had to.

Anyhow, I rationalized, as the man banging his head against the brick wall found out, "it'll feel good when I finally stop."

Everywhere in the world pollution is becoming a growing menace, and even at this distance from the large city of Los Angeles I'd seen evidence of the pollution that this town spews out. On some days, the yellowish smog drifts as far as the mountains, stunting and slowly killing off the pines. At one stage of my journey a vague pall hung in the air and I can recall thinking that there must be a forest fire somewhere up ahead but couldn't figure out why there was no smell of burning…There wasn't any fire of course, it was the insidious poison that was drifting in from the large city that was too far away to be seen itself.

If I had to live in the very source of that pollution, I'd be a bit worried about my breathing gear. It must be a real bummer living in a town where you have to eat your food quickly before it gets dirty.

Passing through the Mill Creek area, I'd kept an eye out for the legendary lost Los Padres gold mines that are supposedly somewhere in the region. They'd been the cause of a rush of hopefuls searching for them in the 1880's.

I had as much luck as them.

Agua Dulce is a small community not too far from the edge of the Mojave desert and I was fascinated as I made my approach to the edge of town. This was the scenery typical of Hollywood cowboy sets, with impressive rock formations rising out of the dusty ground, and not surprisingly, I learnt that Hollywood had frequently used this area for its filming.

It was around here that Tiburcio Vasquez, one of the West's outlaws hid out with his gang until he was eventually caught and hung in 1875. Tiburcio and his men had created all kinds of mayhem throughout Fresno County after being released from San Quentin, taking delight in looting and killing several unarmed citizens.

George Beers, a reporter from the San Francisco Chronicle responded to a large reward offer and led a posse in pursuit of the turbulent Tiburcio. Beers finally wounded the outlaw and helped bring him in to be strung up on the gallows in Sacramento.

As Tiburcio's Mum could well have said, " If you're not careful my lad, them ceegars and Beers is gonna be the death of you."

That incident illustrates the main attraction in American history for me. The hands on, positive action factor of western life. An aspect that didn't lie in the too distant past. Unfortunately though, even in America, you don't get too many journalists riding posse's nowadays. With the cut-backs in emergency and enforcement services, I think I'd feel a little better if allowed to take a more personal attitude in looking after myself.

I made my way through the sandy rock formations heading for the edge of the small settlement. It didn't take much of an imagination...and I was already Clint Eastwood...to picture the ghosts of Tiburcio and his men lurking in the rocks.

Agua Dulce comprised of a post office, small grocery store and a restaurant. There didn't seem to be much in the way of houses around and I wondered how the restaurant could make a living in such a small town.

I made camp in some scrub about a mile from the township, and wandered in to check out the food.

Bartolos was a Mexican restaurant. Good food, good value. I also noted in my journal, "Two beautiful waitresses"

This comment could of course have had something to do with the Second Law of Chauvinism which states, "Female beauty is directly proportional to time and distance travelled."

None the less, up until now, attractive females and an abundance of food were a combination that had been somewhat thin on the ground, and I spent an extra day in Agua Dulce boosting Bartolos weekly take and admiring his waitresses, before eventually picking up my food parcel and hitting the trail once again.

I was heading for Three Points, a small ranching community on the edge of the Mojave desert, 92kms and three days away.

After crossing Martindale and Bouquet Canyons and spending the night at Spunky Canyon, I carried on along the spine of Sawmill Mountain before dropping down to the Upper Shake campground. I could spot no water at the ground, and I approached a large solitary well worn tent to maybe find out where the nearest supply was. There were a group of people living in the tent and their camp looked like a fairly permanent set-up. I think they may well have been semi-permanently ensconced in the area, supplemented by the odd welfare cheque.

They kindly gave me some of their water that they'd carried up some distance remote from their camp, and I sloped back into the trees to contemplate my next move.

Looking at my maps, the trail seemed to wind its way along the spine of Sawmill before dropping down Horse Camp Canyon and do a U turn to double back along Oakdale and Pine Canyon to Three Points. Seemed like a hell of a lot of extra travel to me.

I decided to drop down further through Shake Canyon until I emerged onto a canyon road that would take me through an area marked on my map as the San Andreas Rift zone, leading into Three Points.

I did this, walking through some picturesque woodland and past what looked like an abandoned mine entrance before hitting the Pine Canyon road.

Just before the township I passed by a large official looking county billboard.

"NO SHOOTING" it declared.

I was delighted to see that the local anarchist had been using the letter O's as targets. Their centres almost completely blown away.

Three Points consisted of a one store/diner ranching community. It also marked the beginning of my crossing of the western edge of the Mojave desert, and I figured that it would take me just over two hot days to reach the dusty town of Mojave from here.

Some time before me, in 1826, a bible carrying, rifle toting trapper by the name of Jedediah Strong Smith crossed this desert to become the first American to enter California from the east. Two of the things he had on his mind, were beaver skins and a search for the mythical San Buenaventura River. The river supposedly provided access from the pacific to the Rocky Mountains and would enable ships to reach trappers working in the interior.

Needless to say, he didn't find the river, but the following year he at least qualified for the Guiness Book Of Records, by making his return trip via the Sierra Nevada and Mojave to reach Salt Lake City and become the first American to return from California by an overland route.

He either left something behind or found that beaver skins were a lucrative item, because later that same year he re-traced his steps west back across the Mojave. Only this time he was attacked by Mohave Indians who wiped out ten of his eighteen men.

He still managed to reach the coast of California and headed north towards Oregon, only to be attacked once more, this time by Umpqua Indians who dispatched all but two of the expedition. Jed's luck finally ran out when he himself was killed by Comanches at a water hole near the Cimarron River, just one month before his thirty third birthday.

I wasn't anticipating quite as hazardous a trip, figuring that probably my biggest threats would be from being harpooned by a falling Joshua tree or inadvertently doing a down trou' and squatting on a rattler. Having still not solved the problem of where to put a tourniquet that would isolate such an awkward and sensitive location, I hoped that any disaster was of the former kind.

Somewhere deep below me, at a point where the desert meets the San Gabriel mountains, the San Andreas, Pinyon, and Punchbowl faults were converging in a continuous slow motion collision to create a one to three kilometre-wide subterranean fracture zone. The outcome of this is constant movement, which in turn causes the Mojave desert to slide past the mountains at a rate of fifty millimetres a year.

As far as I was concerned this was good news, as it meant that I'd now be stepping on to a conveyer belt, albeit a very slow one, and all assistance was gratefully appreciated.

If only I was able to hang around for the next 1,355,904 years, I wouldn't even have to walk to reach Mojave town!

I dropped my heavy pack outside at the door and stepped thankfully into the small dining area of the lone store.

Initially, I wondered if something weird was going down. There were about five of the locals seated inside, merrily talking away as I entered. The silence was immediate, as if someone had called out, "CUT!" and they watched me expressionlessly as I uncomfortably checked out the menu on the wall.

"G'day", I tried, "How's it goin'?"

A slight unsmiling nod from one of them, but still no verbal response! I didn't have long hair, it couldn't be that. Maybe I was looking a bit derelict, or had inadvertently broken some unknown Code Of The West.

I looked back at the wall again, trying to think of another stunning opening conversational gambit, when one of them thankfully called out to the invisible proprietor, "You'd better get out here. There's *two* men need feeding!"

They were obviously accustomed to the ferocious appetites of hikers that made it to their store.

The lady appeared, took my order of Chilli beans, and everyone started talking again.

Maybe it was just my appearance or their slow talking way that had caused the silence. Or maybe, "Chilli Beans" was a kind of social password in this neck of the woods - as in, "The guy's okay, he chows down on Chilli beans!"

As I sat in the corner and ate my beans, I was delighted to note that just about all the weathered locals that came into the store were wearing spurs and the typical stetson cowboy hat. Somehow the Kiwi gumboots and black singlet just don't crack it up against that.

I'd mentioned earlier on, that this leg of the Mojave desert was surprisingly no problem when it came to water supply. The reason for this is the Los Angeles Aqueduct.

This is a massive pipeline buried in the desert, and carrying water from the Sierra Nevada all the way to LA. I'd heard that every mile along this line, a small inspection plate gave access to the invisible rushing underground river. I found that with a bit of ingenuity, I could tie a line to the handle of my small cooking pot, lower it through the inspection opening which was only just big enough and then pull up the water-filled pot. Almost as easy as turning on a tap! Each time I did this though, I prayed that the handle on my irreplaceable pot wouldn't break off in the strong flow of water.

There are times when this flow is stopped for servicing reasons. I gambled that my crossing was not going to be one of those times, and my luck held out. So water was no problem. Other legs of my journey were *much* drier!

That was another thing about this trip. It made you realize just how important the basics of life were. Life is just a bit more intense without the convenient, "whoosh" of a fridge door, squeak of a supermarket trolley, or the splash of a tap. Observing the wildlife and insects that this journey put me into everyday contact with, it became obvious that their lives consisted of a continual search for food or water. Unfortunately, even I had joined the survival chain and my food and I were considered to be on the menu for various life forms. Food had also taken on a whole new priority with me, and even though I carried my own it was never enough and I had to discipline myself to keep it strictly rationed. Water was even more important and a source of that once mundane fluid became an essential daily target.

One, "trick" I'd discovered, was performed first thing each morning before leaving a water source. I'd force as much water as possible down myself until I was totally bloated and threatening to explode, then splosh uncomfortably off into the sunrise like a water-logged camel. I found that by doing this I could go for at least five hours before even thinking of drinking again!

The following US Government figures give some idea as to the importance of water. They'd derived these figures using subjects that weren't even carrying heavy packs:

Without water, if you stay put in one spot you can survive,

2 days at 120F, (49C) 5 days at 100F, (38C) or 9 days at 80F. (27C)

If you *walk* during the day, *even without* the weight of a pack, you can cut those figures by one third.

An excellent gauge on your state of hydration, is the frequency and colour of your urine.

Further north in the High Sierra, because of the colder temperatures it was easy to slip into the mistake of not drinking enough. I was aware of that and used this urinary gauge to keep an eye on my fluid intake. Bearing this in mind, a good tip for travel in the High Sierra is ..."Don't ever eat yellow snow!"

I took off in the direction of Mojave, passing the entrances to distant unseen ranch houses.

The Circle C, 4K, and Bar C slowly fell behind me, along with battered, bullet-riddled garbage. Almost continuous wind blasted everything day and night and it was difficult to sleep at nights with the tent rattling away. The Mojave was pretty barren, with the only vegetation being the large cactus-like Joshua trees, their long spines rigid and needle sharp. Incongruously, they are a member of the lilly family. *I'd like to see a vase of them* gracing Aunt Minnie's lounge room table. They can also live for well over 200 hundred years, which was a bit too long to be stuck in the Mojave desert I thought.

The trees were named by the mormon pioneers, who figured that they looked like Joshua pointing to the promised land - punk hairstyles must have been around for longer than we thought.

I experienced my first clumps of tumbleweed blowing along here, jumping involuntarily the first time one of these tumbleweeds overtook me. My brain had caught a glimpse of it from the corner of my eye, thought it was a coyote racing silently up alongside me and immediately did a gibbering somersault screaming out evasion commands. I hastily calmed it down, then chastised it with an imagined newspaper headline,

"Foreigner savaged by rabid tumbleweed."

It's a fascinating piece of vegetation and apparently the idea is that it rolls along wherever the wind takes it, distributing its seed along the way.

I've had a couple of mates over the years who were a bit like that.

Some hikers do this desert stretch at night when the temperatures make for easier going.

I'd considered this but dismissed the idea, as I really don't mind a bit of heat (there speaks a fireman) and also at night, rattlesnakes, sidewinders and other reptilian things like to lie around getting the heat from the ground. I didn't want to go stepping on anything wriggly in the darkness and besides that, I needed to conserve the batteries in my small penlite torch.

I had visions of groping about in the darkness wielding my snakebite blade and severing a main artery whilst the excitable organ in my skull sloshed frantically around gibbering, *"Don't Panic! Don't Panic!"*, like Jonesy in Dad's Army.

The Mojave town edge of the desert was dotted with the usual jetsom of human habitation, and I photographed myself enjoying a comfortable break in an old abandoned armchair.

"Oh yes, I always carry one of these, one can't be too comfortable on the trail y'know!"

The edge of the desert was also dotted with huge windmills that were used to generate electricity into the grid system. They were the same sort of thing that I'd seen further south at Mesa, in the lower Sonoran desert area near the Coachella Valley. As one local with a sense of humour had said to me, "Ain't no wonder it so goddam windy out here. If'n they'd switch off them goddam fans we'd be awright!"

My impression of Mojave town wasn't that brilliant.

It seemed a noisy, dusty, fast food, pass through sort of place, and the winds in the region were beginning to get me down. I've always found that continuous winds eventually wear me down and get me into a bad temper. I used to think that it was a condition peculiar to me alone. Apparently it's not. I read somewhere that continuous winds can produce mood changes in some creatures.

There must be a grumpy load of bastards living in Chicago.

First step as usual was to demolish some calories. The second step was to pick my way through the big rigs clustered around a truck stop and get into a welcome shower. ($5 includes towel, provide your own soap). Then on to the post office to pick up my next load of supplies and get some mail away.

Besides the usual card to Uncle George to prove that I was still alive and HADN'T GIVEN UP, I mailed off a poster to the troops back in Auckland's Devonport Fire Station. It depicted a grizzled, disgruntled weathered looking cowpoke, with the caption, *"There's some things they didn't tell me about this outfit."* I thought they might appreciate it.

I loaded everything up, and headed out of town. A freight train, Santa Fe painted on its wagon sides, pulled slowly past me as windblown grit sandblasted my face and legs. The track ran parallel with the main road and was adding to the bustle and wind that was beginning to hack me off.

A few kilometres into the peace of the desert I thankfully dumped my pack, made camp and set about preparing my evening meal. My staple diet on this trip was porridge in the mornings made from the supply of oats I carried, and a re-hydrated concoction in the evenings. The dehydrated dinners weren't too bad really, but they had the rather bothersome trait of passing through my digestive system rather efficiently, keeping me regular with a precision that compared favourably with Greenwich's atomic clock.

The problem with this regularity, was that it chose to forcefully manifest itself at the first sign of light every morning. The small size of my tent necessitated a crouched exit on all fours and this vulnerable position made for some close calls. Each morning I'd eject from the tent like a ballistic missile, running as far as I dared before frantically digging a latrine hole in a race against time.

This state of affairs carried on for far longer than it should have, until I noticed the pattern and then cunningly began digging the hole *before* I retired for the night. Ah, the joys of camping!

Next day was a long hot one, taking me through a section of the Mojave where the Space Shuttle sometimes lands, and on through Cinco which seemed to comprise of about two buildings and nothing else. Next up, alongside highway 14 was Cantil.

Cantil, on the deserts' northern edge, was not much more than a post office and small general store.

That'll do me. Into the store and into a cold drink.

I sat outside in the shade thrown by the wall of the store, finishing my drink and dreaming of gaining some elevation and maybe a drop in temperature.

A distant rumble materialized into a gang of motorcyclists that pulled to a stop alongside me in front of the store.

They looked the part, Harleys, tattoos, unshaven, biceps and bandannas. I guess they could have been a bit intimidating, but I was feeling a bit too weary and trail worn to care.

The rider nearest me switched off his engine and looked down.

"You walkin'?" The question was asked unsmilingly, and I wasn't sure whether it was a friendly query or a trick question.

I figured that monosyllabic Clint Eastwood type grunts were required here.

"Yep."

"Where you headed."

"Canada"

"Where you come from?"

"Mexico."

I noted with satisfaction, that several of his cohorts heads snapped

round when I disclosed my starting point. This was no mean distance.
"Man that's heavy."

One of the others added, "'Bout as heavy as you kin get."

They trooped past me and into the store, emerging with packs of beer that they loaded up into saddle bags, kicked their bikes into life and pulled out down the highway. The last one out reached into his bag and without speaking, threw me a beer before taking off.

I enjoyed that beer, and shouldering my pack, set off with high spirits into the desert again.

Suddenly I wasn't weary, I'd just impressed a bike gang.

...What more could a bloke want!

Taking a break in the Mojave Desert

Chapter Four

Jawbone Canyon, Inyokern, and Mountain Goat Vern.

Five weeks and almost 970km had passed by now, and I'd grown used to the quiet and solitude that surrounded me when I got away from roadheads.

So it was a shock to be rudely interrupted by civilization for an hour or so outside Cantil. Unfortunately I'd reached the vicinity of a road on a weekend, and that meant weekend visitors.

I was peacefully hiking through the scrub towards Jawbone Canyon. (Bees were humming, birds singing, breeze breezing, rattlers rattling and me thinking).

All of a sudden...*Bloody Trail Bikes!*

Filling the air with noise and fumes, churning up the landscape and breaking into my reverie! Reading from my journal for that day, I'd written in capital letters,

"I HOPE THEY DEVELOP PILES THAT FRAGMENT INTO A MILLION PIECES AND LODGE PAINFULLY IN WHAT THE CRETINS CALL THEIR BRAIN - AND I HOPE THEY FALL OFF!!!

I was becoming intolerant. They were probably quite nice people.

A hot traverse through Jawbone Canyon led into Alphie Canyon and from there the beautiful Buterbredt Canyon, complete with an easy climb up a dry waterfall wall. The lonely remains of a roofless adobe building near a stand of cottonwoods gave stir to thoughts of its past inhabitants, its walls slowly disappearing under the build up of time and sand blown against them.

Butterbredt Spring was to be my next water source, though when I eventually reached it I couldn't be bothered with the hassle of stopping to assemble water filters and fill bottles to add weight to my already loaded pack.

As it turned out, I wished later on that day that I had taken the time.

The surrounding area is now a wildlife sanctuary and I interrupted a photographer who was carefully setting up to get some birdlife shots there. I apologetically and silently detoured to leave him to his task.

A little further on the irony of life struck me, when four stampeding jack rabbits hurtled past me. I entered a clearing and found that what had spooked them was a couple of hunters, father and son, both dressed entirely in camouflage gear and toting shotguns.

I thought of the photographer - totally different types of people interested in totally different types of shot!

I guess that in my day I've been both types, but I've somewhat mellowed with age and unless it's necessary for food, then the hunting and killing aspect doesn't much appeal anymore.

The last mile of that day was spent looking for water.

I'd finished off my last drops some hours before and I was seriously drying out, wishing that I'd taken the time to replenish at the previous springs.

I detoured in the direction of a spring that was marked in Kelso Valley, and camped near a grove of willows and cottonwoods.

Not only was I thirsty, but I was hungry as well and my dehydrated meals also needed water to transform them into something that vaguely resembled food.

I eventually located the, "spring" that was marked on my map. It had been trampled into a disgusting cattle bog.

Evil looking water gleamed up at me from hoof sized indentations. The cattle had also obviously been making their own contributions to the moisture content of this dubious, "oasis".

I couldn't move on, I was too knackered, but I had to drink and eat or I was in trouble, so getting as close as I could to where I thought the spring originated, I cursed the bovine population of America and assembled my water filter. I managed to almost fill a bottle before the brownish fluid blocked up my filter and I sat there peering at the bottle, suspiciously eying my catch.

I was sure I could see Giardia Lamblia formation swimming teams doing the breast stroke across the surface, interrupted occasionally as the typhoid relay team thrashed frenetically from side to side.

I took no chances, boiled up the filtered water and then biffed a couple of purification tablets in for good measure.

If anything survived that, it deserved to survive.

I cooked my dinner, drank the remaining water and awaited results. Thankfully nothing within me exploded, and I drifted off to sleep dreaming of kitchens where the twist of a tap produced torrents of pristine water.

I broke camp at 0600 the following morning in strong cold winds. I was gaining altitude now and beginning to feel like I was eventually approaching the Sierra Nevada.

My right shin had now taken over, "pain duty" from my left knee and I was glad to make camp at 1630 that afternoon at about 6000ft (1829m) in the Sequoia Forests' Scodie Mountains.

My Thermarest sleeping pad had sprung a leak a few days ago, which meant that I was getting thoroughly pissed off at waking up feeling like I was lying on a tablecloth spread over boulders.

I decided that now was the time to do something about it and after a sprinkling of water detected the pinhole leaks, a couple of bandaid plasters from my first aid kit, reinforced with a drop of superglue, solved the problem.

Small triumphs, great rewards!

The following morning presented me with fine weather and easier going and after filling my water bottle at McGyver Spring with its nearby deserted small, "board and batten" cabin, I crossed Highway178 at Walker Pass.

The trail led me round the eastern slopes of Mount Jenkins, heading for the 6800ft (2073m) ridge between Lamont Peak and the Spanish Pinnacles where I'd camp for the night after a thirty four kilometre day and as usual, sore shins.

Indian Wells Canyon stretched out to the east far below me, further east again, the small desert town of Inyokern could just be seen.

I didn't know it then, but I would soon be paying it a visit.

My progress was briefly interrupted at one stage while I dived for shelter and added some more layers of clothing and a pair of gloves. The wind had suddenly increased along with a big drop in temperature - the Laguna Hills experience was still strongly in my mind and I wasn't about to let the wind chill factor get me again!

Two days after this I reached Kennedy Meadows on the edge of the South Sierra Wilderness, but not before putting in my longest day yet. The day before, I'd already pushed myself 32kms through the Dome Land Wilderness to reach, "reliable all year round water".

Problem was, the reliable water was now a dusty creek bed - morale suitably agitated, I drily cursed my way onwards for a further eight kilometres until the crystal clear Kern River hove into sight. For the first and only time during my journey I completely disregarded the wisdom of filtering the water, plunged my head into it with all the vigour of a Saharan legionnaire and blissfully syphoned off a few gallons.

Stuff the giardia.

The approach to the Kennedy Meadows store was as the name suggests, a pleasant one. The going was along gently undulating open country that belied the fact that my next stage would be a climb up into the snowy High Sierras where my average altitude would be around 10,000 ft (3048m) peaking at over 13,000feet. (3962m)

Some time further back, I'd found a paperback, Desert Solitaire by the late Edward Abbey.

Abbey was somewhat of a rebel with a strong love of the wilderness, in particular the Arizona desert areas. He is something of a cult figure amongst the outdoor set, and I kind of liked his attitude.

I acquired an article on him at a later date, and was delighted to read that once on entering the room of a, "high flying" function that he'd been invited to, he had commented to his mate, "Let's get outta here, this place stinks of lawyers."

I could empathise with him there. I've had experience with lawyers, and now some with rattlesnakes.

On the whole, I prefer rattlesnakes.

I could also understand his attitude on the use of motorised transport that some folk use to, "see" the wilderness.

It seems to me that the magical places are the places that are inaccessible to transport, and anyhow, if you're just going to drive somewhere, look, and drive away again, you might as well save yourself the bother and just get a video.

Here's a bit of advice from Edward Abbey.....

"Do not jump into your automobile next June and rush out to the Canyon country hoping to see some of that which I have attempted to evoke in these pages.

In the first place you can't see anything from a car; you've got to get out of the goddamned contraption and walk, better yet crawl, on hands and knees, over the sandstone and through the...cactus.

When traces of blood begin to mark your trail you'll see something, maybe."

His book Desert Solitaire was a good read, so I carefully deposited it in a conspicuous but sheltered spot and hoped that some other, "distance" hiker might find it and get some enjoyment out of it.

I finally arrived at the Kennedy Meadows store to find Ziggy and the Gimp comfortably ensconced and eating their way through the store's stock.

My food parcel from Trail Foods had also duly arrived before me, and I spent most of the remainder of the day reloading my pack with it and also adding some extras that I managed to salvage from the duo's feeding frenzy.

I eventually managed to cram everything into and onto my pack and along with the water I would have to carry, discovered that it now weighed a bone-compressing 100 pounds (45kg).

There was no way that I could swing the damn thing up onto my back without fear of either breaking a harness strap or rupturing my Foo-Foo valve.

After several experiments, I perfected a technique of sitting on the ground and working my way into the pack harness. Then I'd draw my legs up under me, get onto my hands and knees and then slowly struggle into an upright position. Another technique was to manhandle it up onto a rock of appropriate height, harness myself in and stagger off in an upright position.

I mused at the advice given me regarding what to do if confronted with a bear.

"Don't run", I was told.

Right, no problem mate, I could hardly bloody walk!

I had also been expecting a parcel from Ziggy's sister Allison. I'd been a bit concerned about the adequacies of my sleeping bag and thought that it may have been a bit too light for the conditions up in the Sierras.

I couldn't afford another bag but reckoned that a sleeping bag cover, which is a good deal cheaper, would add a bit of extra insulation.

Allison was to have purchased one for me and mailed it on. As yet there was no sign of it.

Ziggy too was awaiting a supply parcel from her.

We approached the store lady.

"Where does the mail get sent here from?" Maybe the stuff was sitting there.

"Inyokern."

Ziggy gave a groan. Inyokern, the nearest town, looked like a two day walk away.

A two day walk was nothing to either of us, but not in the wrong bloody direction, we were migrating North!

Incongruously, for all our escape from civilization, time had become an obsession with us. The reason was that every day lost on the trail, meant that we were a day closer to winter and its heavy snowfalls at the northern end of our journey. Unless we averaged out the entire journey at around twenty seven to twenty eight kilometres a day, then chances were we'd end up bailing out because of snow conditions.

The store lady picked our obvious dismay, "I'm goin' into Inyokern sometime tomorrow, I'll call at the mail office and pick anything up for yuh."

We thanked her, and headed off about a mile down the road to Irelan's diner, returning that evening to make camp near the store.

The following morning we left our gear at the store, and the lady dropped us off at, "Grumpy Bears", a bar some miles down the road that was holding a BBQ.

"No need to come into Inyokern" she assured us, "I'll pick up any stuff and see yuh later."

The bar was in full swing, plenty of beer, and impressive chunks of incinerated barbequed meat.

The locals were into horseshoe throwing contests, and off to the side I was intrigued to see a sign proclaiming, *"Chicken Shit Raffle"*.

An area had been fenced and the ground marked off in small squares, each with a number. You bought a ticket with one of the numbers on it, and then watched as an indignant chook was set down in the arena. The square that received the first chook turd was declared the winner! The punters on the sidelines would frantically attempt to shoo the celebrity chicken towards their square, which was itself a gamble, as any sudden noise invariably precipitated an unrehearsed bowel movement!

Ziggy approached me from out of the crowd looking less than happy, "I've just seen the storelady. I asked her about the parcel and she said she'd forgot about it!"

FORGOT! This was serious stuff!

What a fuckwit! We were both royally pissed off, and even though I kept reminding myself that this was marginally better than being pissed on, it did nothing to alleviate the mood.

We discussed the situation and decided to hitch straight away into Inyokern.

It was 4pm on a Saturday. We might just get there in time if the Post Office stayed open in the afternoon.

We clambered into the back of a pick-up and were soon deposited in town.

The office was closed - damn. That meant a wait until Monday, unless the manager lived locally (it was a small town) and we could explain our situation and persuade him or her to open up for us.

We asked in a nearby shop if anyone knew where the PO manager lived, but with no luck.

I was sitting downcast in the gutter when two policemen in a car cruised by. I could see the cop in the passenger seat turning to watch me as the car did a right turn and headed away from me on the other side of a vacant lot.

I had a sudden inspiration, maybe the police would know where the manager lived! I stood up and waved at the distant car.

They must have been still watching, for the car did an immediate turn and headed back. It didn't occur to me that I may have looked something of a derelict, but without my backpack, covered in grubby trail clothes and close to two months beard growth, I suppose I didn't look too savoury.

I was surprised as the police car, instead of pulling up alongside me and parallel with the sidewalk, swung out and turned in nose towards me, some distance from the sidewalk.

The cop on the passenger side got out and still standing behind his open door, beckoned me closer. The driver meanwhile, had also stepped out of the car, and had circled around until he was at about a 45 degree angle behind my right shoulder.

I was beginning to suspect that this was not going to be straightforward.

"What's your problem?", unsmiling.

I glanced quickly over my shoulder, curious to see what his partner was doing.

He also stood there straight-faced and watching closely. He sported a No.1 haircut and rather resembled a uniformed, unfriendly pit-bull.

I gave the officer standing behind the car door the full story, but there was still no relaxing of attitude.

I don't know what was going on in his head, but I was getting the impression that they were thinking I was more interested in robbing the PO than picking up a parcel.

"No, we don't know where the manager lives, prob'ly over in Ridgecrest. Got any ID?"

Luckily, I had brought my passport with me, and he studied it closely.

"How'd y'say yuh got here again?"

I told him the whole story over again, along with a detailed explanation of why the parcel was needed. He remained unsmiling, but I thought that I finally detected a slight relaxing of attitude, as his partner had by now come round to my field of vision.

"Sorry, we can't help yuh."

Ah well, at least I've convinced them that I'm a good old Kiwi on a hike, and not an axe murderer or something.

They got back into their car, and just before they pulled away, the cop who had been interrogating me looked unsmilingly up at me,

"You sure yuh ain't wanted or missin' or nothin'?"

Maybe I should have a shave.

Ziggy had disappeared into a store and I was standing outside at a mechanical newspaper stand - I was wanting a twenty-five cent piece for the machine and after checking the few nickels in my hand, realized that I didn't have enough coin.

No problem, under my T shirt in my money belt was a couple of hundred US dollars and some travellers cheques.

I was just about to turn to get some change in the store, when a man passing by stopped. He pressed a quarter into my hand, "Hell, you'll have your paper, ain't nothin' but a quarter!"

I thanked him for his kindness, and away he went.

I really should get a shave.

Ziggy returned and we discussed our next move. We decided that all we could do was to get into a motel for the next two nights, then pick up the parcel first thing Monday and hitch back to Kennedy Meadows. We took off down the street heading for a motel, and spotting a bar, decided to stop off for a beer.

There were only two customers in the small bar, both drinking and playing at the pool table. The younger of the two, a man in his thirties, struck up a conversation with us. He was interested in where we came from and where we were going.

He was drinking fairly heavily, "Why don't you stay at my place. I live on the edge of town and you're welcome there. Got showers, food, clean bed.

"Thanks for the offer."

"I only got a small car though. Can only take one of you out at a time."

He looked at me, "I'll take you out then come back for your buddy."

A warning bell rang somewhere in my head.

"That's all right, we'll just get a motel, thanks all the same."

He began getting persistent, all the time insisting his car was too small for the both of us.

"Must be a bloody small car", I commented.

"I think he fancies you", muttered Ziggy, "Looks like the kind of guy that would have guns. Probably lives out in the desert somewhere. I'm not going anywhere with him."

"Why don't you just give us your address and we'll see you there?" He didn't like that idea.

"I've had all sorts of folk stay over at my place, why don't you come?" He was drinking more and becoming more assertive.

"No thanks mate, we'll give it a miss, thanks all the same."

He was becoming agitated and his voice had taken on an aggressive edge, "What's the matter with you guys? I'm offering you my hospitality!"

Now, I find it hard to be abrupt or assertive to people who are being pleasant to me, but this guy had just crossed himself off the list. My voice raised, "WE DON'T WANT TO COME!"

I was getting close to telling him where to stuff his freaking hospitality, along with a set of pool balls and his glass of beer.

"Let's get going", said Ziggy.

"Good idea."

We left him muttering about ungratefulness. The other guy hadn't said a word all the time we had been in there.

I was getting a bit paranoid about my appearance by now, so I was quite relieved when we were shown a motel room by the friendly smiling proprietor. I'd half expected him to start yelling, "Get out! We ain't having no bums in here!"

The motel room had a television set in it. Quite a luxury, I'd forgotten that they existed. I randomly flicked on a channel.

It was a TV evangelical preacher in full flow. I'd never seen or heard one before and at first I thought it was a comedy programme spoof. But no, the guy was for real. I couldn't believe the glitz and bullshit!

How could people take him seriously?

Apparently some did though, *and* sent him money!

We lay there on our beds, cleaned up and stomachs full.

"This is the life", said Ziggy.

"Yeah", I replied, "Stuff the workers."

"As my old man would say", said Ziggy, " We ain't nothin' but a couple of turners."

I was curious, "What's a turner?"

Ziggy grinned, "A turner is someone who does nothing but lie around turning food into shit!"

I should have known, the explanation jolted my memory back to my days at sea.

Our cooks were usually known as, "fitters and turners". The theory was, they fitted food into a pot and then turned it into crap.

We were round at the PO first thing Monday morning. Sure enough the parcel was there - we grabbed it and headed out to the road that would take us back up into the hills and Kennedy Meadows.

I tried thumbing a lift with no luck, so we decided that we might have a better chance if I sat at a discreet distance and the more presentable youthful Ziggy tried his luck.

Sure enough, first vehicle to come along stopped. Ziggy piled in with the driver and I climbed up onto the deck of the pick-up.

I was beginning to feel like a dog or something. I really really should get a shave.

Kennedy Meadows was my last available supply point before reaching Reds Meadows 328kms away through the High Sierras. I was carrying enough food for 18 days, plus the extra equipment and water that I would have to carry - Ice axe and crampons were now part of my load.

Ziggy and the Gimp had left earlier, and I set out alone just after midday.

I said farewell to the storelady (whom I now no longer really felt like talking to) and asked her if any other hikers had gone through on the trail ahead.

"There's an old guy on his own somewhere up ahead. Went through a couple of days ago."

I noted the information and promptly thought no more of it.

The pack was numbingly heavy, making a team effort with gravity to try and flatten out my knee and hip joints.

I trudged slowly through Pinyons and Jeffrey pines, before thankfully making camp at Crag creek about eleven kilometres further on.

The Sierra Nevada, along with parts of Washington, were to prove to be the scenic highlights of the journey, although the desert areas of the south had appealed very much to me as well. They had possessed their own special brand of stark beauty, dotted with brilliant cactus flowers and inhabited by unfamiliar reptiles.

I met hikers further north who told me that they wouldn't hike through the southern desert areas, as they were apprehensive about the heat and the lack of water. I had found that as long as I carried enough water, then these areas were no threat. On the other hand I was to find that further north in the mountains, where you could experience snow and extreme cold conditions at any time, things could take on a much greater urgency. Even with the proper equipment and clothing, at times you had to be prepared to utilize it quickly for it to be of value, and there was the ever present threat of snow which was not only cold but covered trails and reduced visibility.

Up until the mid eighteen hundreds, the Sierras had enjoyed comparative serenity from human interference.

The Indian tribes, of which there were five main groups: the Sierra Miwok, Yokut, Maidu, Washo and Mono, along with the early Spanish missionaries and explorers, as well as American hunters and trappers, had very little impact on the area.

However, in January 1848, things changed in a big way.

James Wilson Marshall discovered some gold nuggets at a place called Sutter's Mill on the American river.

This kicked off an international gold rush, and within two years there were about 50,000 miners, all trying to strike the big one in the range. This of course led to a bandwagon of supportive facilities like banks, retail stores, transport, agriculture and industry.

The men and women of this rearguard were probably the smart ones, as I'm sure that out of the 50,000 miners, the vast majority must have given up with little more than enough money to drown their sorrows or to buy their fare home.

By 1880 most of the interest in mining the area had waned, but there is still some mining going on in places along the 150 mile Mother Lode system that stretches along the western reaches of the Sierra Nevada.

The start of the Sierra Nevada also meant the start of bear bagging! Bear bagging was a pain, it entailed stuffing all your food supplies and anything else aromatic (toothpaste) into a bag, and each night hauling that bag up a tree.

All agencies strongly recommended doing this - The tree should be as far from your camp as you can reasonably locate again.

The bag should hang at least 6m off the ground and 3m out from the main trunk. (An optimistic requirement in some areas)

No cooking should be done in or near your tent.

Bears are scavengers, and if they smell anything like food in your tent then they're likely to come through your tent looking for it - if you're in there at the time, (and they're mostly nocturnal) you're going to need a lot of Elastoplast.

For about the next 3200kms I'd be in bear country.

California, Oregon and Washington are a habitat of the Black Bear, a full grown adult weighing in at around 180 - 270kgs. Although called

Black Bear, they can range in colour from black to a cinnamon or brown colour.

I was told that they wouldn't usually bother you personally, unless you were between him and his (or what he considers his) food or between her and her cub.

The bad news was, they have been known to attack and kill humans, and if they do feel like a bit of bother, they can easily out-run you, out-climb you and generally ruin your day. They are capable of killing an adult deer with one swipe of their paw.

Grizzly bears were a different matter again, potentially far nastier and much more unpredictable.

All the advice on what to do in grizzly country seemed to be a bit contradictory. "Use bear bells", was one bit of advice - bear bells were small bells that you could attach to your boot, pack or hiking pole if you used one. The bells would jingle as you hiked along, giving the Grizzly advance warning of your approach.

The theory was that you then wouldn't surprise the bear. Apparently they don't like surprises, and tend to rip your head off if you give them one.

The problem with that theory, is that I'd heard stories of them stalking hikers.

If that's true, then merrily walking along playing, "jingle bells" would have every hungry grizzly in the neighbourhood converging on you like kids chasing a musical ice cream van.

Besides that, I felt it would be particularly un-cool to wander around with little bells tied to my boots like a woodland Noddy or an itinerant Morris dancer.

Luckily, there wasn't any chance of meeting up with Grizzly Bears until I reached the extreme northern end of Washington, and then I was told, only a very remote chance. I hoped that the Grizzlies knew this.

Another nightly ritual I was to perform from now on, was to urinate in a circle around the outside of my tent.

To get around the entire tent, usually meant urinating at a trot, (see, girls can't do *everything*) or perfecting a sort of stop start method.

This anti-social mobile flash was for the purpose of laying down my scent. I'd heard from various sources that it may act as a bear deterrent - I was willing to try everything!

As it turned out, I was to be harassed in my camp on three separate nights by bears. On one night providing them with a nocturnal nosh-up, after they grew tired of monstering me and diverted their attention to walloping my remaining food supplies.

I also made two daytime sightings, one a bit too close for comfort. Besides these actual sightings, there was always plenty of evidence of bear activity in some areas. The only other animal that may have proved a hassle was the mountain lion.

I didn't see one, though did sight what appeared to be mountain lion tracks - or those of a rather big moggie!

I'd finished my evening tucker and decided that now was the time to hoist my gear up a suitable pine tree.

I broke out the line that I'd carried specifically for this event, tied a rock to the end of it, and after a couple of attempts managed to hurl it over an upper branch.

I didn't use my separate "bear bag", but instead lashed my entire pack to one end of the line. I couldn't be bothered unloading and separating the edible and aromatic from the rest of my stuff.

It was a mistake.

I held the pack up as high as I could, then gave a mighty heave on the end of the line.

Nothing happened.

Shit!

The pack hung there at shoulder height, like a dead weight of treats just awaiting the next teddy bears picnic.

Okay, this calls for maximum muscle! I took a deep breath and gave a mighty heave.

Crack, Twang!

The branch above me had given way under the pressure, the pack and the branch landed on top of me and I was reduced to a disorientated heap, joining my pack in an embrace as we rolled down an incline, coming to a halt with a sore head and a grazed knee.

"Bugger the bears", I thought, and crawled into my sleeping bag.

I awoke early the following morning to the alarm on my wristwatch, glad to realize that neither my food nor myself had been visited by bears, cooked up my porridge, broke camp and was on the trail again by 0615. I was quite excited to feel that I was finally approaching the High Sierras.

The trail followed the sometimes dry Crag creek, passing an old Indian trail that led off to the eastern Owens Valley, a route that was once considered as a possibility for a trans-Sierra railway. Thankfully it didn't eventuate.

Becks Meadow, Cow Canyon, corn lillies, mountain bluebells, all interspersed with boulders, Lodgepole and Foxtail pines, absolutely beautiful country.

I was now in altitudes consistently over 10,000 feet (3048m) and as interesting as it was, I was beginning to feel the weight of my pack. I'd reached a flat forested ridge, and through the trees, glimpses of various peaks could be seen. Olancha Peak, Mount Langley, Kern Peak.

This was all very nice but I was starting to sag and even though there was no water up here, my mind was beginning to turn to thoughts of a campsite. I plodded on, occasionally lifting my gaze from the trail to study the route ahead.

I looked up... there was someone up ahead sitting at the side of the trail. I caught up to him and he stood up to greet me.

He looked to be in his sixties and must have been, "the old guy" that the storelady had mentioned.

"Hi! The name's Vern otherwise known as, "Mountain Goat!""

We fell into step and got into conversation.

"G'day, my name's George otherwise known as knackered!"

We talked further and he mentioned that he'd spent a vacation doing a bit of hiking in the South Island of New Zealand some months ago.

Something clicked in my head. No, surely it couldn't be the same person.

"Your surname isn't Anderson is it?"

"Yeah! How'd you know that?!"

This was too much of a coincidence!

I looked at him, "We know each other, we wrote to each other about five months ago!"

The world is surely a small place. Five months ago, John Tuke, a fellow firefighter and keen cyclist, had been on leave and cycling around the South Island.

He came across Vern, "Sitting by the side of the road in the middle of nowhere and whittling away at a stick."

John knew about my pending walk in America and also that I was considering buying some of my equipment when I got to the States, as it might be cheaper there. When he found out that Vern was an American, he'd asked if he minded if a friend of his wrote to him with some questions on equipment prices. Vern had been more than willing and had given John his temporary New Zealand address to give to me. I had duly written to Vern while he was still in New Zealand, and received a very helpful and friendly letter in reply!

This was spooky. We pondered the odds that would have allowed us to meet up on the other side of the world and be at one particular remote spot on one particular mountain range at the same time.

We were both amazed, and decided that it must have been ordained that we meet!

Vern had done the first part of the Crest trail a few years ago, and was now having a go at the remainder.

The chance meeting had recharged my batteries, and we carried on together to find a campsite with some water. We eventually left the South Sierra Wilderness, crossing into the Golden Trout Wilderness, and about three or four kilometres later made a good campsite alongside a small creek.

I know it was a creek, because I got a good look at it by being too exhausted to prevent myself from falling into it as we crossed to better ground. I'd done over thirty hard kilometres that day and when I stumbled on the uneven rock bed of the creek, the weight of my pack which would have still been over ninety pounds, proved too much to counterbalance and down I went.

Vern helped me and my damaged pride to my feet, "I reckon you're gettin' a bit tired."

Ziggy and The Gimp had turned up, and after swapping a few trail experiences, I excused myself to crash into my tent and pile up a few Z's.

The next morning the others made an early start. I called out that I was still recuperating and that I'd see them sometime later as I was still a bit tired.

This was only partially true.

I actually wanted to walk alone. As good as their company was, four would have been far too much of a crowd with too much talking.

Just one companion is enough really, and then only for brief periods. I kind of enjoyed the solitude and knew that I'd see much more wildlife by travelling alone.

Besides, as Rudyard Kipling said, "He travels fastest who travels alone."

I eventually left at about 0700 and a mile or so later lost the trail - ominously enough, near Death Canyon.

Maybe in my case, Kipling's saying should be amended to, "He travels fastest who travels alone, but not necessarily in the right direction."

In my defence, it's fairly easy to lose the trail in some parts and frustratingly, even though I had copies of topographic maps for the entire journey they were only strip maps. That means the maps only illustrated the area on average, three to four kilometres on either side of the trail. Consequently, if you got lost and wanted to locate yourself by reading the map and taking a bearing of a mountain peak or land feature that was say six kilometres or more away, you were out of luck. Generally the trail was easy to follow, but there were times when I would have dearly loved a full map. The reason that I nor most people don't carry full maps for a journey this long, is the old bogey weight, plus the inhibitory cost factor involved.

I spent quite some time casting around trying to relocate a trail, was unable to recognize any features that were on my map and eventually decided to backtrack to where I *knew* where I was and start again. This time paying more attention.

Like most people I guess, I can plug along handling most conditions as long as I know just where I am and where I'm heading - which is probably a good analogy for life, really.

As far as hiking goes, when I don't know where I am, my mind tends to jump around a bit with a preference to landing on the more negative scenarios.

Things like, "Oh no, I'm going to wander around 'til I run out of food, freeze to death or fall down something and break a leg!" Moments like these certainly focus you.

True to form, I looked around at the unfamiliar woods and pondered the fact that I was now in Sasquatch territory.

Sasquatch, or Bigfoot, is the North-west American equivalent of the Yeti.

He's supposedly a large hairy creature, six to twelve feet tall, standing erect on two feet and often giving off a foul smell.

He sounded like someone I once knew. I'll have to find out if he ever

92

went hiking in the States.

I backtracked and started off again, this time carefully studying my map and distances. I found that this was always the best thing to do rather than carry on compounding any mistakes.

Sure enough, I found the trail again. It had shot off to the left. Obscured under patches of snow, I had missed it and plodded on straight ahead.

Back on course, I was a happy camper again. I decided to have an early day and at around 1530 headed into Dutch Meadow where I found some water and made camp.

I left the next morning at 0600. There was surprisingly little snow around, even at elevations of 11,200 feet. I knew that snowfall was a critical factor in the success or failure of my ambition to complete the distance to Canada off-road. Snowfall can vary from year to year, particularly further south. I knew that I would be heading towards more snow, but so far I was lucky.

On through Cottonwood Pass, traversing the southwestern slopes below 12.900 feet (3932m) Cirque Peak, finally leaving Golden Trout Wilderness to enter the Sequoia National Park at 11,275 feet.(3437m) Another boundary crossed!

The vast Sequoia National Park has an area of 1,863 square miles (4,826 square km) and is noted amongst other things, for the impressive giant sequoia redwood trees that grow within its boundaries. It's also popular for hunting the bear and mule deer that live there.

I smiled to myself as I remembered the advice given to me by Clive Robinson, one of the firefighters on my watch.

We'd been listening to a documentary illustrating the firearms problem in America, and the number of its citizens that were accidentally killed each year during the hunting seasons.

Clive had turned to me and said, "Well George, the only advice I can give you, is don't pack your fur coat or your antler hat."

The park was established in 1908, and was named after Sequoyah, a part Cherokee, and creator of the Cherokee Indian alphabet. Sequoya was born around 1765 and was the son of Nathaniel Gist a British trader and a Cherokee mother. He was raised by his mother in the Tennessee country and never learnt to speak, read or write English. He was however, adept as an artist and also as a warrior, serving with the US Army in the Creek War in 1813-14.

Sequoyah was convinced that the key to the white people's superior power was written language, which enabled them to accumulate and pass on more knowledge than was possible for a people whose mode of communication was dependent on memory and word of mouth.

To this end, around about 1809, he began working on a system of writing for the Cherokees, believing that the increased knowledge would help them maintain their independence from the whites. He first experimented with pictographs, and then with various symbols that represented the syllables of the spoken Cherokee language.

Twelve years later by 1821, he had finally created a system of 86 symbols, representing all the syllables of the Cherokee language.

He then went on to convince his people of the usefulness of his written language by transmitting messages between the Cherokees of Arkansas (with whom he lived) and those of the east, and by teaching his daughter and other young people of the tribe to write.

The system had been uncomplicated and made for easy learning, and before long Cherokees were publishing books and newspapers in their own language.

Good on him!

He sounded like the sort of man that fully deserved commemoration of some sort.

I was making progress towards my goal, chipping away at the distance. The gradual descent provided good views of the Great Western Divide as I dropped further to make my way around the northeastern boundary of Siberian Outpost, named for its desolate aspect.

Later on I got views of Mount Whitney on the boundary line of the Tulare and Inyo counties. At 14,494 feet (4418m), Whitney is the highest mountain in the adjoining United States, and I'd been toying in my mind as to whether to take the slight detour and climb to its summit.

It's not a particularly difficult or technical climb and as the spot where I would have to make my decision was already at 10,300 odd feet it wasn't as if I would have to start at ground zero.

As it turned out, when the final decision time came I decided against it - the pull towards Canada was too strong and I felt that I should channel all my energies into my objective. I had a long way to go as yet, and it was demanding all my resources.

Maybe it was just as well that I didn't - I heard later on that there had been a couple of fatalities when lightning had struck the hut on the summit. There had been a group of people sheltering there when the lightning hit.

The unfortunate hikers who were killed had been sitting on the floor in the hut with their backs touching the walls. My informant wasn't sure of the exact date, but it had been very close to the time that I was contemplating an ascent.

At 0630 I left my camp at Rock creek, passing through stands of lodgepole pine and juniper and continuing on along the eastern slopes of Mount Guyot. This area was littered with the debris of broken mature trees, shattered in a previous avalanche. The younger more supple trees, that had bent under the onslaught, had survived.
There must be a proverb in there somewhere.

I wasn't to witness any avalanches here, but I'd seen a couple back home in the Mount Cook area and their power is awesome.

They make a sound like a fifteen storey building collapsing, which I guess is what they are equivalent to.

Up and over another pass at 10,920 feet, then zig zagging down to carry on and eventually meet up with the John Muir trail about seven kilometres later.

At last! The John Muir Trail! You can't write about the Sierra Nevada without paying some homage to John Muir.

Muir was a Scot, emigrating to the States in 1849. He was probably one of the first conservationists, and vigorously lobbied the US government to adopt a forest conservation policy. He had a true love of the mountains and would spend weeks wandering around in them, from all accounts supplied with not much more than bread and tea leaves. I thought that my diet of dehydrated food was unvaried enough. Though going by the price of the stuff, even if it had been available to him at the time, being a canny Scot, I doubt whether he would have been interested.

I can remember once passing through his hometown of Dunbar, an ancient town complete with ruined castle, picturesque harbour, cobbled quays and fisherman's houses. I'd stopped off at a pub to get a lunchtime meal, had given my order and handed the money to a somewhat bemused barmaid.

One of the locals sitting at the bar had turned to me and said, "Och, I can see that ye're English, paying fae yer meal when ye hav'ny even got it yet!"

Besides his time in the Sierras and walking the wilderness areas of Oregon and Washington, John Muir had also walked from the mid west to the Gulf of Mexico, his journal being published after his death in 1914 as, "A Thousand-Mile Walk to the Gulf."

In 1897, President Cleveland designated 13 national forests to be preserved from exploitation, but businessmen, probably the equivalent of our Business Round Table (may a thousand fleas infest their dwellings and their gold danglers turn to rust) induced Congress to hang fire on the proposal. Two persuasive magazine articles were then written by Muir in June and August of the same year, and completely swayed public and Congressional opinion in favour of the move.

I reckon he had his finger right on it. He was a thinker too. Here are some of his words….

"How hard to realize that every camp of men or beast has this glorious starry firmament for a roof! In such places standing alone on the mountaintop, it is easy to realize that whatever special nests we make - leaves and moss like the marmots and birds, or tents, or piled stone, we all dwell in a house of one room - the world with the firmament for its roof - and are sailing the celestial spaces without leaving any track."

The trail ascended to a high saddle then made its way amongst the huge boulders of a glacial moraine, from where I could see the Sierra crest from 13,990 ft (4264m) Mount Barnard, north to Junction Peak. The temperature had dropped noticeably during my ascent, but the drop was due to the invigorating keenness of mountain air and even though the sky was grey, it didn't look like a snowfall was pending - I hoped!

A rather wet crossing of Wallace creek was made, to be rewarded by an impressive panoramic view from the Bighorn Plateau. Tyndalls creek was another damp experience and I squelched and dripped my way up until I reached a point about half a mile past a side trail that led down to Lake South America.

The weather was beginning to close in now, and some rain had started along with the ominous crashing of thunder. I was at 11,200 feet (3414m) with more climb ahead of me, so decided that now would be a prudent time to make camp. I'd already done a respectful 26 kilometres. Earlier on I'd spotted a lone boot print that looked like one of Vern's, so I figured that he must be around here somewhere and was probably no longer in the company of Ziggy and The Gimp.

Being able to recognize boot prints was one of the delightful discoveries of the hike. I'd never aspired to being The Great White Tracker, but discovered that I had become familiar with the different characteristics of boot soles! Most people had a sole print characteristic to their boot alone, and after months of studying the ground for trails and tracks, I found that I could easily recognize them. Just like animals, each person made a specific track.

This was all well and good, but I realized that my *animal* recognition skills were still a bit on the shakey side when earlier that day I'd ascended a small ridge, to look up and spot what looked like a medium-sized polar bear just above me.

This was a bit disconcerting, as...

a) anything with the name *bear* attached to it can flood my body with dangerous levels of adrenalin, and

b) if it was a polar bear then I was seriously off course.

We both came to a halt, the white shaggy-haired thing turning its head to survey me carefully from over its shoulder.

It wasn't a polar bear of course. It was probably a hornless mountain goat or a mountain sheep. I was to see another of these creatures before the day was out, but still couldn't figure out what the hell they were.

Recalling my lounge room dreaming of being the lone cowpoke/ Indian fighter/trapper, I mused that all I had to do now was poke a cow, fight an Indian (maybe a friendly arm wrestle would qualify) find out what the White Hairy Thing was, and I'd be practically there!

A movement way down below caught my eye - it was Vern! He looked like he was casting around for a campsite. I bellowed out at the top of my voice between the claps of thunder, "VERN!" (Crash of thunder!!)

He stopped, looking around him.

"VERN" (Another crash of thunder!!)

He looked all around again, but still couldn't pinpoint where the voice was coming from.

The poor bugger must have thought he was being summonsed from above, what with all the celestial accompaniment that was going on. There was a huge rock nearby, I figured that if I stood up on that he might spot me.

With a wary eye at the heavens, I scrambled to the top of it and waved furiously, "VERN!" (Crash of thunder followed by flash of lightning!) Stuff that, I dived for ground level and looked up to see that Vern had also done a disappearing act. I hastily pitched my tent, biffed some dehyd into my pot, brought it to the boil and got it down me. All that remained now was to hang my bear bag up a tree. I got the line over a suitable branch, lashed my bag to it and gave a mighty heave.

"Twang, Snap, Thump!"

The line had broken! Damn!

Frustrated, I picked the line up, tied it together again and then noticed that the fall had split open the bag. Bugger! I hate it when that happens! I stitched the thing together again and then with as big a heave on the bag that I could muster, with one arm on the line and one under the bag, I hoisted my pantry up into the thunderstorm.

…I hate bears!

360 degrees of isolation

Climbing to a pass

Chapter Five

Snowbound passes and a meeting with Ursus Americanus.

I was packed and moving upwards again by 0630, there was still no sign of Mountain Goat Vern but I figured that he'd no doubt eventually catch up with me.

Thankfully, the weather had cleared and as I passed above the timberline, the snow-covered terrain levelled out slightly at just over 12,000feet. Looking ahead past two small frozen lakes, I could see the looming massive granite and snow covered wall of the divide.

Forester Pass, the highest point on the trail and my immediate target, stood out like a small notch against the skyline.

My immediate reaction to the awesome sight was, "How in the hell am I going to get up there!"

It looked impossible, unless you were Sir Edmund Hilary or one of those White Hairy Things.

"Hi George!"

I looked around and there was Vern heading up towards me.

"G'day Vern, what d'you reckon?"

He stood looking up at the vast obstacle, "Can't see any trail and it looks damn steep."

I agreed, but people do get over it, so I reckoned that if that was the case, then we could.

We moved off again, closing slowly on the snow shrouded granite wall where we began to discern a zig zagged route upwards.

Progress was slow and we simmered with adrenalin, both conscious of the fact that if we came to grief, then there was no one who was going to report us as missing for quite a while.

Higher up, we met with continuous icy snow, and my ice axe came into its own as I cut steps for us in the hard packed snow surface across a near vertical avalanche chute that dropped several hundred feet below us.

The axe was indispensable, without it the route would have been extremely dangerous, if not impossible.

I was totally focused, averting my eyes from the steep slope below me and concentrating only on cutting the steps as I carefully shifted the weight of my pack, fully aware that one slip and I'd be into a one way ride.

This tricky crossing was eventually followed by the traverse of a narrow icy ledge, then a climb of a thankfully short but near vertical snow wall, to gain the top of the pass.

That last steep snow wall was a worry - I had visions of it falling away, sending me into orbit and collecting Vern on the way.

With a heavy pack giving me the profile of a Sierra Nevadan Quasimodo, I wasn't too keen on these balancing acts, though old Quasi had seemed to flit around his belfry agilely enough.

We finally gained the top without mishap, and flopped thankfully onto the snow.

I was glad to see that we wouldn't be having to climb down any vertical snow walls on the other side. Although quite steep, it wasn't going to present any obvious difficulties.

13,198 feet! The border between Sequoia and Kings Canyon National Parks.

"Well", said Vern, "Now it's easy. It's all downhill from here to Canada!"

Theoretically he was right, the altitude where the trail would eventually enter Canada was 9000 feet or 2743 metres lower than the pass - unfortunately there was going to be quite a few up and down bits before then.

To reach the Columbia River that separated Oregon and Washington, the trail would have to drop over 13000 feet from here!

The High Sierras are spectacular, everything I imagined them to be! Stretching as far as the eye can see in a seemingly endless chain of snow-clad peaks, snow and granite rising in places to over 14000 feet. "Una gran sierra nevada", a great snow covered range, is what Spanish missionary Pedro Font recorded in 1776 when he first sighted them. Right on Pedro!

The year that I traversed them was a comparatively mild one as far as snow was concerned, but even then I was to encounter enough of the stuff to satisfy me.

Regardless of the amount of snowfall on the lower slopes of the range, the mountain passes have snow on them all year round, which is not surprising as many of them stand at around the 3505m (11,500 feet) mark.

We took a short break, throwing some chocolate bars and salami down our throats before beginning the descent down into Kings Canyon.

The descent was an interesting combination of fast, slow, and painful. We took off at an exhilarating speed, glissading down the upper slopes, light-headed in the fast and furious descent that was the antithesis of our climb up to the top of the pass.

All too quickly our progress became bogged down in soft snow as the incline decreased and we struggled along, sometimes sinking waist deep as we lost elevation and the sun softened up the snow.

My shins began to hurt excruciatingly again with each step and scramble forward, and once more my painkillers came into play along with hopes that I wasn't doing any long term damage to my bits.

Snow travel is best done in the early hours of the morning while the surface is still stable and firm. Later on, the sun gets to work and softens things up making travel in deep snow much more difficult. There were to be a whole series of passes that would have to be crossed from now on, almost one a day, and I found myself falling into a pattern of travel that best dealt with them.

My daily routine would be to approach as near to a pass as was comfortable and safe to make camp and then while the snow surface was still firm, set off for the top of the pass at first light the following morning.

I would then make a descent to the other side and head towards the next pass, where the process would be repeated over again. Even if I reached the lower slopes of a pass fairly early in the afternoon, I would still call it a day and make camp.

I realized that to push on would only become an arduous slog through soft snow, burning up more energy and calories than was necessary and taking far longer than need be.

We continued a gradual descent that lay about midway between Mount Stanford and Mount Keith, traversing high above the western shore of an unnamed lake that we could see below us.

We were to lose even more altitude, and eventually double back to ford Bubbs Creek that was fed from this unnamed lake that was lying at 12,248 feet.

All the lakes at these altitudes appeared to be either frozen or partially so, and I was reminded of a grim tale that had been related to me of a hiker that had come to grief on one of them.

He had been hiking in snow conditions and at the end of the day, had made camp and retired to his sleeping bag.

Unbeknown to him, he had flaked out on the frozen surface on the edge of one of the lakes.

His body had been recovered still in the sleeping bag.

The surface had eventually given way under the weight and heat of his body. I can only imagine the horror of waking up to the icy grip and tangle of the sleeping bag - not a pleasant way to go.

After a few more fords of Bubbs Creek we reached pine trees, and after fording Center Basin Creek that flowed from Golden Bear Lake almost 200 metres above it, we tracked along the eastern bank of Bubbs Creek until reaching Vidette Meadows. The creek quietened as it widened out here and made an excellent campsite, overlooked to the north east by the impressive Kearsarge Pinnacles. We had only done about 20 kilometres that day and Vern had decided to carry on, heading for the next pass where no doubt I would catch up to him.

I was to learn that although Vern's pace was a lot slower than mine, he had incredible endurance and would put in long days, sometimes hiking 48kms a day, which with a heavy pack is damn good in any terrain - on one occasion I'd camped the night with Ziggy and The Gimp and we'd spotted Vern still plodding north at the end of the day in an almost trancelike state.

The Gimp had picked up on this and that night as we lay in our respective tents, the stillness of the night was suddenly broken with the loud crackle, hiss, and squeal of radio static as The Gimp tuned his walkman radio over empty wavebands, punctuated by urgent announcements of ...

"Earth to Vern - Earth to Vern, over" ... (crackle..hiss..squeal) ... *"Earth to Vern - Earth to Vern, over!"* ... (crackle..hiss..squeal)...

The moment was totally hilarious, and I still can't hear radio static without smiling and being immediately transported back to the woods and a Louisiana accent.

This was to be my campsite for the night though, 9600feet up in the Sierra Nevada - I was exhilarated, alone and content.

Of all the passes in the range, there are three that stand out vividly in my mind when I look back on my time in the Sierras. Forester, Glen and Muir.

The following morning Glen Pass was my objective.

After Forester, I felt sure that any others would be a piece of cake. However, Glen Pass was about to prove to be rather more difficult than I had imagined.

By 0630 I was on the trail again and heading for the pass that lay just over eight kilometres away and 2,378 feet above me at 11,978ft. (3651m)

An arduous climb out of Bubbs Creek canyon via its north wall took me to easier going along a saddle high above Charlotte lake to my east. A moderate and then gentle ascent finally brought me to the foot of the pass.

Again, as with Forester, it was difficult to discern a trail that led to the notch that was my target - this was mainly due to the fact that a cloudy mist was thickening and beginning to cut visibility.

I switchbacked upwards, the temperature dropping noticeably until suddenly I was at the top.

Usually on gaining a Pass, you could see all below stretching out ahead of you. With the aid of your topo' map you could then visually sight where you intended heading (any trails were obscured in these areas because of snow) then go for it. However, by now visibility had deteriorated even further and by the time I reached the top, was down to about 2 metres max.

There I was on top of the pass, everything was white and cold with no sign of a trail leading down - I noticed that my cowardly brain was slowly edging itself towards shelves full of files marked, "exposure" and "lost", and quickly checked that poltroon with some rational thought. I could either,

a) Pitch my tent up there and wait for the visibility to improve.

(That didn't appeal, what if the weather worsened? It certainly felt like it could start snowing again at any time.)

b) Retreat the way I came to await better weather.

(That didn't appeal either, it was too bloody hard getting up there!)

c) Study the map, cross my fingers, then head off on compass bearings.

I decided on the latter.

I'd been "postholing" along for some time when I heard a shout from behind me.

Out of the whiteness appeared a couple of American hikers. I must admit I was quite pleased to see them, and looked forward to a bit of local knowledge and encouragement.

I'd expected something like, "Yep, you just carry on the way you're going 'til you reach a lake, hang a right and you're there!"

It wasn't like that. What I got was a nervous, "Boy are we glad to see you, we've been following your footprints."

"Don't follow me, I'm lost too!" I replied.

It was sort of meant as a joke, but it failed miserably and they didn't laugh.

We plodded along silently for a while longer, the terrain getting alarmingly steep, disappearing into a thick blanket of whiteness.

I noticed that they were becoming more hesitant and beginning to lag behind.

After a mumbled discussion between them, my two brief companions informed me that they had decided to retreat back over the pass before their prints disappeared and await better conditions.

They were probably right, but I decided to carry on, after all, I had to reach Canada didn't I!

I pushed ahead, staring at my compass and contouring down the steep snowy slope. Next moment, as I struggled to lift my leg up out of the snow to make my next step, I lost my balance, the weight of my pack pitched me forwards and suddenly I was into two downward somersaults followed by a short skid and then another somersault. As I acrobatically made my way north, I remember hoping that this route didn't end up in any sudden drops. I finally came to a halt, and sat there imagining a panel of judges holding up their score cards. 7, 8, 8, 7.

"Quite spectacular, but we feel his landing let him down."

Luckily I hadn't damaged myself, but an item of equipment hadn't been so lucky. I had a pedometer attached to my waist belt under my jacket. It was a small watchlike gadget that registered the number of steps you took and then translated them into mileage.

The casing had snapped making it inoperative. It had been very useful to me earlier on in my journey, as it greatly assisted me in knowing just where I was. If you knew reasonably accurately how far you'd walked, then in conjunction with the details on your topo' map you could get a pretty good idea of your position.

I must confess that I was pretty pissed off at breaking a good bit of gear, but it wasn't such a big deal, as by then I could do a pretty good assessment myself of how far I'd travelled over any particular terrain.

Before leaving home I'd received some tuition on map reading from fellow firefighter Jan Bottimer. Jan is a member of the Territorial Army and as such, was adept at using a map to get himself around off the beaten track.

I'd mentioned at the time that I was taking along a pedometer.

"Not a bad idea", he'd said, "But after a while you'll find that you won't need it."

He was right.

The weather, assisted by the lower elevations had started to lift by now, and just as I started off again I was halted by another call from behind.

It was Vern! He'd followed my tracks, passing the other two hikers as they'd made their way back. Vern had made his camp at the foot of the southern side of the pass and somehow I'd got ahead of him. We carried on together, until a small frozen lake came into view.

We skirted the edge of the lake while I studied my map and compass. I reckoned that if we headed northeast from here we'd eventually strike a creek that fed down into Rae Lakes and close by we should pick up the trail again. I made this navigational announcement with more confidence than I felt.

108

I'd come to realize that the longer I live, the more often I'm wrong! This time though I was right. We located the trail, visibility finally cleared, and we found ourselves at the beautiful Rae Lakes.

I sat on the rocky shore of the southern lake content that my map reading had worked, and hauled out some bread and salami.

The surroundings were superb, with the reddish and purple banded colours of rocky Painted Lady, a peak that towered above the southern tip of the lake, patched with snow.

Vern had taken off to have a go at catching a trout or two - the trout were quite colourful, though to my taste had a rather bland flavour. Vern was a bit of an expert at catching them and I think he supplemented his diet quite often with them.

As an emergency measure, I carried a hook and line and a small jar of salmon eggs as bait, but I seldom took time to fish unless I'd happened to finish for the day at a likely spot. Even then I was usually too knackered to think of much else but a quick meal and my sleeping bag.

A movement on the rocks nearby caught my eye. It was to be the forerunner of my first close encounter with a marmot!

These were yet another new experience for me and welcome but cheeky visitors - the furry creatures, around 20 inches long, were a ground dwelling rodent and a member of the squirrel family. They lived in the rocks, hibernating in winter. I don't think they were long out of hibernation at that time, so they were quite hungry and very cheeky. This one slowly got closer until he was alongside me and my pack, then began pulling at the bag that held my food. I rescued the bag from him, offered him some bread, and he ended up eating out of my hand!

I noted as my journey passed through summer and autumn, that as they got fatter preparing for winter, they also presumably got less hungry than this fellow and therefore would never approach as closely again.

They were really cute characters, like little fat men in fur coats and in the course of my journey they were to become a memorable part of my social circle, dining with me, amusing me, and allowing me to hold one sided conversations on such profound issues as The Meaning of Life and The Attributes of Pamela Anderson.

It wasn't exactly, "Dances with wolves", but it was safer and much more fun.

Vern had by now caught a couple of trout, and after bidding farewell to a slightly fatter and less hungry marmot, we crossed the isthmus between the lakes and tracked along the pleasant and gently descending trail on the eastern side. After Arrow Lake, Dollar Lake and several fords later, we reached Woods Creek where a wooden bridge spanning the flowing water was going to make for an easy crossing. We decided however, to leave that for the morning, and made camp for the night.

We sat around the small fire that Vern had made, waiting for the billy to boil. Vern was very quiet and looking thoughtful, and I sensed that he wanted to say something.

"You know George, I wouldn't have gotten over those passes if you hadn't been there."

"Yes you would."

"No.... I was wondering if we could do the next pass together in case it's like Forester."

Although I think we both enjoyed the solitude of being alone in these environs, I had no objection to his suggestion.

Vern had no ice axe and attempting a pass like Forester without one would be dangerous if not suicidal. As for his being impressed with my navigation off Glen Pass, the success of that had been due more to stubbornness, an overriding desire to make progress north, and plain good luck.

The spot we were camped at was apparently quite popular with hikers, although we had it to ourselves that night as it was probably too early in the season for the majority of people. Its popularity was testified to by the presence of two large ominous looking steel boxes with heavy lids. This was the only time that I was to come across this facility.

The idea was that you sealed your pack in the heavy duty steel box to protect it from bears. The thought crossed my mind that a better idea would be to seal yourself in the box, and leave out a sacrificial snack for the hairy guys.

Dinner that night was somewhat more nutritional than normal, as Vern had added his fish to the pot - for once my stomach had a pleasantly full feeling about it!

We cleaned up our gear, bade each other goodnight, deposited our packs in the steel boxes and retired to our respective tents.

I didn't know it then, but that night was to be my first close encounter with a chap known as Ursus Americanus - The Black Bear!

I didn't know what time it was, but it was dark, and something had woken me up.

I lay there listening, when a sudden deep growl from somewhere not far beyond the foot of my tent almost sent me into cardiac arrest. This was followed by a rapid shuffling and a higher pitched growl that now came from the side of the tent.

Jesus H. Christ! Bears!

Not just bears, but a bloody bear and its cub!

From everything I'd read, this was the worst possible combination. What if the stupid cub came bouncing into the tent, spotted me and told its mum!

I lay there thinking, "Should I yell and frighten them off?"

I decided against that.

With a cub being there, a yell might put momma into attack mode and anyhow I suspected that a yell from me at that particular moment would come out more as a wimplike squeal.

Besides, I noted that Vern, who had more experience of the American outdoors than I did, was apparently lying in his tent definitely not yelling.

The playful growling of the cub progressed to the space between our tents. This was immediately followed by a huge and horribly pissed off roar from the adult who had now prowled around to the head of my tent.

This was *terrible*, I was *scared* and would have gladly traded off a months food for an elephant gun or something of similar calibre.

The growls and roars went on for what seemed like an eternity, until suddenly they weren't there anymore.

I cautiously peered out of my tent...they'd gone.

Needless to say, there was some pretty fitful sleep that night and they returned once more before the dawn, just in case we'd managed to drop off to sleep.

We were probably part of the regular entertainment for the bears - "Hey Yogi, what yous guys doin' tonight?"

"Dunno Bruno, how's about we take young BooBoo here down to Woods Creek an' give them campin' dudes a fright?"

We broke camp the next morning, thankful that we'd had the use of the steel bear boxes.

Further north, I was not to be so lucky.

Our day began with a steady climb, following the northern bank of the creek and passing tortured pines that had been gnarled and twisted by the weather. Finally the grade eased off somewhat, and we reached the junction of Sawmill Pass trail that disappeared eastwards.

Somewhere off to the east of here, bear-free and probably oozing pancakes and maple syrup, was the small town of Independence lying slotted between the Sierras and the Inyo Mountains.

It was almost worth a few days detour!

There was no shortage of water in this section of the trail, and we made several fords of icy creeks before swinging westwards along the creek that formed part of the headwaters of the Kings River, named originally by Spanish explorer Gabriel Moraga, as Rio de los Santos Reyes. River of the Holy Kings.

Bounded on three sides by the majestic peaks of Crater Mountain, Mt.Wynne, and Mt.Perkins, we turned north to begin our ascent to Pinchot Pass on the western side of Mt.Wynne.

As usual, the views from the top of the pass were spectacular, at 12,130 feet we gazed on mountain wilderness as far as the eye could see! We were both relieved to find that there was not as much snow present as was on the previous passes, and after a short break began our descent to the lake filled valley below. The weather was fine and clear now and with summer under way, if there were no future prolonged bouts of snowfall, then there should be just enough of the white stuff around to become the aesthetic icing on the cake!

Vern and I parted company here, and I settled down amongst lodgepole pines to enjoy my surroundings and take a break.

"See ya later George - watch out for them bears!"

I waved goodbye, and after allowing sufficient time to build up a bit of space, I hit the trail once more.

I finally made camp for the night at around the 11,200 foot mark, two and a half kilometres from Mather Pass and surrounded by beautiful scenic snowy mountains.

The climb to Mather Pass was rewarded by views to the north and northwest of the impressive peaks of the Pallisades group lying along the boundary of Inyo and Fresno counties.

I had gained the pass early in the morning. As yet, the sun hadn't had a chance to do its work on the surface and the snow on the steep descent was still very icy and firm. I decided that if I tried glissading down the slopes, I'd probably end up imitating a toboggan. Alternatively, if I cut my way down using the ice axe it would take ages.

This called for crampons. I strapped them on, and headed off feeling very expeditionish - George of the Antarctic sallies forth!

Now, walking in crampons requires a certain technique as it is very easy to, "can out" if you're not careful or familiar with them.

I was familiar with them all right, but therein lay the problem. I was just familiar enough to get myself into trouble!

I headed off down the slope full of the joys of summer.

This was excellent, with the help of the crampons I was sticking to the side of the pass like an alpine fly, progressing at an impressive rate of knots and admiring the scenery.

Before I knew it, I was admiring the scenery at ground level, still progressing at an impressive rate of knots but with the subtle difference that my face was now being used as a snow plough.

This was definitely uncool, and I was glad that only the Sierras and myself were witness to my close-up inspection of their snowy surface. My headlong descent was brought to a painful halt when my shoulder hit something solid, swinging me around and putting me into a good position for an ice axe arrest and a jet of snow up my nostrils.

What had precipitated this ride, was one of my crampons getting hooked up in my opposite overtrouser leg as I strode adventurously forward.

I sat there in the snow nursing a sore shoulder, an egg-like lump on my head, and a lump-like ego on my Id.

Paying much more attention, I safely reached the gentler ground of Palisade Lakes and then began the switchbacked, "Golden Staircase" descent down the thousand foot rocky cliff gorge of Palisade Creek.

The trail took me due west along the north bank of the creek, fording Glacier Creek just east of Deer Meadow and continuing on through pine forest where towering granite slopes rose from the side of the trail reducing me to the significance of an ant.

Needless to say, after the rigours and acrobatics of the preceding days, most parts of me were in pain by now and I decided that being in such idyllic surrounds I would take an early day for some R & R.

I pitched my tent next to a crystal clear running creek in pines and aspens, surrounded by magnificent rocky mountains.

The sheer vastness of these granite walls made pines growing near them look like dwarfed bonzai plants. Sometimes the natural grandeur of the Sierra Nevada could bring a tear to the eye, they were an emotional as well as physical experience for me, and there were many locations there that I would have dearly loved to have been able to spend more time in.

I sat by the edge of the creek, taping up a crack in my plastic cup that had succumbed to my dive off Mather Pass and realized that since leaving the Mexican border, I hadn't given a toss about any of the material things that I'd left behind in Auckland.

My house, car, computer and other possessions that had been so important to me, were for now at least, completely meaningless.

All that I needed was what I carried on my back.

I felt very together, my only allusions to insanity, apart from the fact that I'd walked this far, were the brief one-sided conversations that I held with my absent mate Blackie.

Being a cat, I figured that he was probably telepathic, he certainly knew when I was thinking of food.

Anyhow, I rationalized, it was less suspect than talking to myself.

I looked at my watch, it was only 1445 and I'd clocked up only eighteen and a half kilometres since my last campsite, but the sky was blue, the sun was warm, and I was alone and happy.

I left the following morning at daybreak, continuing west for a short distance before heading northwards into Le Conte Canyon, its steep walls showing signs of avalanches that had crashed down from its heights cutting a swathe through the trees.

A movement caught my eye, and I managed to get a photograph of a stag as he stood watching me carefully before he disappeared amongst the trees in the dim early morning light.

The canyon was also home to a grouse and her chicks that scurried away to safety on my approach, leaving a chipmonk to watch me curiously. I felt like I was an extra wandering through a nature film-set in one of Disneys' stories.

Maybe that's how the Le Conte Canyon got its name - The Story Canyon!

...Either that or some disgruntled Frenchman hadn't thought much of the place.

On past Little Pete and Big Pete meadows then a swing west again and finally the climb above the treeline to Muir Pass, the gateway to get me through the Goddard Divide.

Muir Pass at 11,955 feet (3644m) proved to be another physical and emotional test.

This pass was different from most others, in that once gaining the top it carried on into the distance on a near level plain before finally descending steeply into Evolution Valley.

As I gained the pass, a picturesque domed stone hut came into view. This was the Muir hut, built in 1931 and looking like a stone version of a Mongolian yurt or something that would have looked more at home in the mountains of Tibet!

The pass was completely covered in snow and the subsequent lakes I passed were frozen. Half a day was spent "postholing" across this area. Just about each step causing me to sink almost to my waist in snow.

My pack was heavy enough without having to struggle out of a snow hole with every step, so I tried to alleviate the situation a bit by taking off my pack and dragging it behind me on a line.

I figured that this would make me lighter and I wouldn't sink down as far. This idea was only partially successful, as the effort required to drag the pack was just as bloody tiring!

I gave up and resorted to carrying my pack once again.

Taking a break, I looked back to sight a distant figure heading

116

towards me - it was The Gimp!

I knew that he had seen me and as a joke I dropped down behind a snow covered mound in pretence concealment. It appealed to my sense of the ridiculous that anyone would think that after two people had sighted each other, one could then conceal himself in such a pristine white, vast and open place! Especially as my tracks through the snow made it totally obvious where I was. I would have stood out like the proverbial dogs' goolies!

My sense of humour backfired a bit though. The Gimp came into view, peering down at me from atop the snowy mound, a sort of exasperated and hurt look on his face, "Hey man, what'ya hidin' from me for?!"

I explained that I was only having him on, indulging myself in one of the strange vagaries of antipodean humour.

He looked at me suspiciously and gave an unconvincing, "Oh."

It was the truth, I hope that he believed me.

The Gimp reckoned that Ziggy was up ahead of us somewhere, and I assumed that Vern too was somewhere ahead, though the, "Mountain Goat" had the knack of popping up where you didn't expect him.

We struggled on together, skirting frozen McDermand and Wanda Lakes. Wanda Lake, like Helen Lake just before the pass, was named after one of John Muir's daughters.

Bit of a frigid namesake I thought - for the sakes of any contemporary suitors I hoped that the actual daughters had possessed a warmer disposition.

The frigid lakes were followed by a fording of Evolution Creek that ran from the northern end of Wanda Lake and a descent into the Sapphire Lake basin, trudging past the lake that gave the basin its name. To the east making up the Divide, were a series of tremendous but cold and unwelcoming looking peaks, each named for evolutionary thinkers - Darwin, Spencer, Haeckel, Huxley, Wallace.

The man responsible for their naming was Theodore Solomons, a charter member of John Muir's Sierra Club. In 1895 he'd climbed up into this basin and after studying the peaks, had written in his journal,

"I felt that here was a fraternity of Titans that in their naming should bear in common an august significance. And I could think of none more fitting to confer upon it than the great evolutionists, so at one in their devotion to the sublime in nature."

I did some evolutionary thinking myself, and whilst not quite as flowery as old Theodore, came to the conclusion that I was evolving into the august significance and sublime nature of an under-nourished packhorse.

We were headed for the northern end of Evolution Lake, where according to the map, the contour lines spaced out nicely signifying level ground. This was always a major issue with me. I hated trying to sleep when I kept rolling into the side of the tent, or slumping to one end of it like a disgruntled barrow load of wet concrete.
A few extra minutes selecting a level site were always worth it and I'd pay as much attention to selecting my patch of dirt as your average shopper would pay to selecting the family bed.

We were both pretty tired by now and being tired you tend to make mistakes.
Our mistake was to traverse the western side of Evolution Lake instead of its eastern side.
Looking at the map, it was obvious which way we should have gone, but we didn't, and instead of wandering along fairly level terrain we found ourselves in steep snow and struggling belly down up over a snowy bank to avoid icy water. We were both almost completely drained of strength and energy by now, and our blood/sugar levels must have been batting zero.
The Gimp looked wearily at me, "Man, this motherfuckin' Pacific Crest trail tests you every goddam inch of the way."
I agreed wholeheartedly.

118

We eventually reached the northern end of the lake and made camp in the snow at about 10,850 feet.

We could see the warmer hospitable wooded Evolution valley over a thousand feet below us, but we were both too tired to consider the descent. Even the Gimp was not his usual cheerful talkative self, and believe me, that meant it *had* to have been a hard day!

After a quick meal, too tired to clean out the pot, I crashed into the damp warmth of my sleeping bag and lay there savouring the lack of mobility, the crossing of another pass, and contemplating my journey so far.

The amazing thing about this adventure was the *contrasts*.

From deserts, hills and heat, to mountains, snow and chill.

From light-headed euphoria, to downhearted despondency.

From easy as a stroll in the park, to a breathless gut-busting struggle.

From *always* feeling hungry, to overflowing with hashbrowns and pancakes!

Much later, some people would look at me incredulously when they heard about the walk, and say something like, "Whatever did you want to do that for?!"

After a while, I wouldn't even try to explain. The fact that they had to ask that question meant that they would never be able to understand. I knew why.

Every day was a physical and mental challenge, *but every day I had a goal and a sense of achievement.*

Every day was spent in country where it felt like it *meant* something to be alive.

Every day the vastness and remoteness of my surroundings brought home my insignificance and made me realize that I had no more *right* to life than a marmot, an ant or a rattlesnake.

Every day reinforced the realization that it was the *basic* things that really mattered.

Every day taught me to appreciate and be thankful for *small* things.

At the end of every day I was *content* and *happy!*

And if that wasn't enough, to top it off, I'd been told that I *wouldn't be able to do it.*

So for what they are worth, those are just seven reasons why I, "wanted to do that."

The next morning the Gimp was up before me. "Think I'll get going and try catch Ziggy up.'

"Okay mate, see you later."

I waited a few minutes before struggling out of my warm bag to face the cold. This was closely followed by a realization that fate, or more truthfully my own stupidity, was giving me another little test, when I found my boots and socks frozen solid.

Tired, I'd made the mistake of leaving them in the vestibule of the tent instead of inside with me. Beating your socks on a snow covered rock so you can get your feet into them is *not* a happy moment!

After making the steep descent, Evolution valley proved to be excellent walking, apart that is from some falls that I took fording tributaries of Evolution Creek. The majority of these had to be crossed by hopping icy boulders or doing a balancing act across fallen trees. I didn't have much luck with my boulder hopping and a combination of slippery boulder, worn boot tread and heavy pack, had me crashing into the icy waters on a couple of occasions, luckily without too much damage to myself or equipment.

You had to hurl yourself at the damn things with total commitment and hope that your boot wouldn't skid off or the momentum of your pack didn't overbalance you. I hated boulder hopping and wasn't to be so fortunate in escaping injury further north.

The log cabin at McClure Meadow that served as a ranger station proved to be locked up with no sign of a ranger.

I'd heard that this was a summer station and as it was now mid June, I'd assumed that he would have been in residence, and had been looking forward to talking to someone who would have known something about the area.

Too bad, maybe he was out ranging.

Heading northwards along the South Fork San Joaquin River, I eventually reached Piute Creek, where the Piute Pass trail carried on northwards following the creek. I headed west, entering the John Muir Wilderness and leaving Kings Canyon National Park carrying some good memories along with my load.

A steep climb up out of South Fork Canyon and I made camp amongst pines, once again in substantial snow at about 10,000 feet (3048m) and four kilometres from Seldon Pass.

It had begun snowing as I prepared my evening meal on a stove that had started spluttering, farting and going out when the will took it. This behaviour had started several days before and I had made a mental note at the time to give it an overhaul when I next took a break. Typically, along with a couple of other small things that I'd promised attention to, it still hadn't been seen to.

You'd think that with nothing to do but walk all day, an hour's additional break would be no big deal, even welcomed.

Well it wasn't like that. I seemed to have this compulsion to keep moving, and unless I was stopped to check out something, eat, sleep, look at a map or attend to some necessary bodily function, I couldn't stop myself from, "pickin'em up and puttin'em down"!

I knew why. I was too aware that I *had* to average those twenty seven to twenty eight kilometres a day for the entire trip if I was to reach my goal. As far as I was concerned if I didn't reach Canada, no matter how many miles I had covered, I would have failed. Subsequently, I'd always promise myself that I'd attend to my failing stove when I made camp. Then when I'd made camp I'd be too knackered to bother, and put it off 'til the next break...and so on.

Tomorrow I would *definitely* overhaul it!
I bear-bagged my food and hit the pit.

I awoke the next morning to discover that my small tent felt even more claustrophobic than usual...it had snowed heavily overnight, practically burying my tent. The weight of the snow had compressed the roof until it was just inches above me.
Surprisingly, it was quite warm in there, must have been an igloo effect!
I lay on my back and kicked upwards, clearing the snow before crawling out into a beautiful white world.

Despite the heavy snow, I had no real problem locating the 10,900ft (3322m) pass or the eventual descent from it. The only worry that did befall me, was a dense cloud of fog that rolled silently and menacingly upwards behind me as I made my ascent through the deep snow surrounding Heart Lake. With memories of Glen Pass still strongly in my mind, I put on as fast a pace as I could muster, trying to gain the pass before being overtaken in whiteout.
The fog seemed almost a living entity as it silently dogged my footprints, blanking everything out as it came.

I just managed to outpace it for the half mile or so up to the pass, and was rewarded with marvellous views of Marie Lake and the mountains beyond.
The fog, which still filled the valley below me to the south, seemed to have worn itself out in the race to the pass and slowly dissipated as it reached a point just fifty feet below me.
I gave it a two finger salute and started off down the other side.

I got a lot of satisfaction out of the Sierra passes. Besides the fact that each one marked off another milestone in my trek north, they each also provided stunning views of the seemingly endless wildernesses that stretched ahead and behind me...The north to be experienced, the south to be remembered.

Chapter Six

Sadie's Important Message, More bears, Yosemite's Postal Employee From Hell, Little Norway.

By the end of the day, the weather had turned to an overcast drizzle, and I switchbacked down off Bear Ridge to make camp at 7,750 ft (2362m), about nine kilometres and 3,150 ft (960m) below my next objective, Silver Pass.

I coaxed my stove into life, persuaded it to cook my Louisiana Beans & Rice, then crawled into a damp tent and equally damp sleeping bag before drifting off to sleep, punctuating the still night with minor explosions courtesy of the Louisiana beans.

0600 the following morning was very cold and after gaining the pass through the usual snow, descended past a veritable tribe of lakes - Chief, Papoose, Warrior, Squaw and Lone Indian Lakes.

I was taking a break at Purple Lake when I met John.

He'd commented on my trail worn appearance, and was impressed when I told him where I'd started from - I in turn was impressed when he told me that up until recently he had been in the US Army.

He was extremely fluent in Russian, and his job had been to listen in to Russian military radio traffic.

He'd become quite familiar with the voices of some of the operators and had gradually been able to build up a personality profile on many of them. Most of the traffic was run of the mill stuff, but he had intercepted the occasional interesting piece of information.

He must have spoken the language like a native, so I was intrigued to find out that although he would have dearly loved to visit Russia, he never had. He had been prevented from doing so by the very nature of his job.

Maybe with the passing of time and hopefully the continued lessening of tension between the two nations, he may someday be allowed to.

We finished off a beer that John had provided, then we parted company and I made a descent down into the pleasant Cascade Valley where I picked up the Rainbow Falls trail and made camp in the woods. It was here that I eventually sorted my stove out.

A bit of time spent cleaning the jet and replacing a leather pump washer did the trick - it was my only replacement washer, so I hoped it was going to last the distance.

It was here too that to my shame, I monstered an aspen tree in the name of romance.

I don't usually subscribe to the idea of carving away at trees, but absence as they say, makes the heart exceeding fond and the romantic idea of leaving Sadie's name carved deep in an American woods appealed to me.

However, by the end of the next day, after 'phoning her from Mammoth Lakes, I was feeling like I would have rather left *her* deep in an American woods.

After a frustrating early morning search for my polypropylene gloves, I set off for Reds Meadow gloveless. I looked high and low for those damn gloves but never found them. I *know* I had them on when I stopped the day before to make camp but they had somehow vanished. There had been no wind over that period, so they couldn't have been blown away.

My only theory is that somewhere in the Californian wilderness, a smug marmot is complementing his fur-coated elegance with a nifty pair of paw warmers.

Acting on information from a pack horseman that I met later on in the morning, I made a short detour with the idea of enjoying a natural hot spring that steamed seductively in the vicinity. A quiet relaxing soak sounded like a good idea - I immediately canned the notion however, when I arrived at the spring to discover half a dozen yelling teenagers had beaten me to it.

I was obviously closing in on civilization now, so with the consolation that this would mean food, I headed off once more in the direction of Reds Meadow.

I reached Reds Meadow early in the afternoon.

The sudden burst upon this small resort was quite a culture shock after talking mainly to trees and marmots for so long - a cafe, a store, cars, campervans, sightseers and day hikers resplendent in colourful, "hiking" clothes with jaunty day packs.

I couldn't help feeling a bit superior as I scruffed past them out of the woods, finally looking like an, "outdoorsman" and no doubt smelling like something that would be best left outdoors.

My first priority of course, was a meal at the cafe.

The next was to check if any mail had turned up at the store/mail office. It had, along with a short, sharp, cryptic letter from my girlfriend back in New Zealand.

"Call me when you can", it had said, "I have something important to talk about."

This immediately set off a whole barrage of alarm bells ringing in my head. When a female says something like that and not much else, it does not bode well.

It could only mean,

a) She was pregnant.

b) She had met someone else.

c) Someone had persuaded her that a footloose fireman who tends to wander around in the woods is not a good bet.

d) She'd been watching Oprah Winfrey or Ricki Lake (which could mean *anything* was bothering her).

e) All of the above.

I immediately decided that my best plan of action was to hitch into

Mammoth Lakes.

From there, I could make a 'phone call to discover The Important Thing, attend to some gear maintenance, then do some serious eating, followed possibly by some serious drinking depending on the nature of The Important Thing.

A couple of guys that I recognized from the Packhorse station wandered past and I asked them the best way to get to Mammoth Lakes.

"In the back of our pickup!"

They were headed into town, and I gratefully accepted their offer of a lift.

Mammoth Lakes was a fair sized settlement, having most things a hiker could want. I checked my watch, noted that I should wait a few hours before calling NZ and looked up and down the street in search of a camping store that might have a spare washer for my stove.

"Howdy George."

It was Vern! He'd got into town a few hours before me and was looking for somewhere to get his pack fixed or something.

After attending to our shopping needs, our thoughts once more turned to our stomachs.

"C'mon George, let's get into this restaurant and I'll buy you Prime Rib, puts real power in your legs!"

I protested that he didn't have to pay for my meal as well, but Vern insisted, "I was treated real well by folk during my stay in New Zealand and this way I feel like I can repay that kindness a little."

I couldn't argue against that, so in we went!

The aroma of cooking food along with all the accoutrements that went with it was almost overwhelming, and we drooled our way to the nearest table.

We were attended to by an attractive young waitress, and Vern, twinkle in his eye, put in the order, "Two Prime Rib's rare, two beers, and are you looking for a boyfriend?"

The young waitress took his query good-humouredly, "Naw, you guys are hopeless, here today and gone the next. I'm looking for something more permanent."

"Ah well, worth a try Vern!"

The meals were excellent and we stepped out into the street pleasantly bloated, to spot Ziggy and The Gimp headed towards us.

"Hi guys!"

"Hi Vern, Hi George, foreigner, ain't yuh!"

We decided that we'd be staying the night in town, and the four of us checked into the local Motel Six.

The time had eventually come for me to ring NZ, so loaded with a mountain of coins I dialled and waited with baited breath.

"Hello"

"Hi, it's me, got your letter, how's it going?"

"Never mind how it's going! Why did you give Janet your car and why are you using her camera?!!"

So that was it!

To me, the explanation was logical and innocent.

Janet and I had divorced amicably about five years previously, and I hadn't sighted her for about four of those years.

She had since re-married, but used to ring me up about once a year to see how things were going.

She knew nothing about my pending journey, but had happened to make one of those calls just before I was due to leave on my trip.

I'd told her about my plans and mentioned that I wasn't sure what I was going to do with my car, as I didn't want to particularly leave it unattended at my place, and Sadie didn't have garage space.

Janet had spoken to her husband, and he'd said it was okay to leave it with them, as it'd be under cover and they'd give it a run now and then to keep things working.

When I'd dropped the car off at their place, Janet had offered me the loan of a camera that was small, had a self-timer, and was light and foolproof, so I took it.

I hadn't mentioned any of this to Sadie, as I didn't want any unnecessary feelings of insecurity being stirred up and if she didn't know, it wouldn't bother her.

As far as I was concerned, I'd seen my ex for the first time in about four years, solved two problems that had been bothering me and that was it. I promptly forgot all about it.

Wrong move!

Apparently Sadie's sister had met my ex in town one day, they'd talked, and the news of my heinous crime had grapevined back to Sadie. As far as she was concerned, I was now an uncaring, unfeeling, untrustworthy lowdown form of pond life, and there was no reasoning with her. Tempers ran high, coins ran low, and I slammed the 'phone down on her.

I stood there in the 'phone booth feeling quite revved up and very alone. Gave it some more thought, became even more frustrated and indignant and deciding that I didn't deserve or need this, headed off darkly in the direction of a bar to rendezvous with the troops.

"Give this guy a beer, he's just fallen out with his girlfriend!"

It was the beginning of the end of a beautiful relationship.

Give me marmots anyday, all they worry about is food and where their next pair of gloves are coming from!

I was feeling slightly fuzzy-headed for most of the next day and later on, deciding that we'd had our fill of civilization for a while, we hitched a lift to about fifteen kilometres from Reds Meadows. It was getting a bit long in the day now, but the others carried on down the road heading for Reds Meadow and the trail, hoping to maybe get another lift.

I decided to call it a day, and pitched my tent in the trees near the side of the road. The stop was useful anyhow, as it gave me some time to re-stitch the ankle seams on my boots and to re-shuffle the damaged brain cells in my head.

I was back on the road fairly early the next morning, and was lucky to hitch a ride back into Reds Meadows with the owner of the cafe there. I made a comment about the free coffee that seems to get supplied in all the US eating houses. It was a novelty to me, as at that time there were very few NZ places that would part with a cup for much less than two dollars. Here you had to sometimes practically beat the waitresses off to stop them topping up your cup.

I wasn't complaining, but sometimes my self-discipline leaves a lot to be desired and I floated out of several diners feeling like I'd been mainlining caffeine.

The cafe owner assured me there was a bit of cafe psychology going on here. All to do with tips for service and the fact that for the few cents the coffee cost the owner, you'd end up hanging around and spending more.

As a long distance hiker and therefore constantly in a state of advanced hunger, I wasn't really in a position to confirm his theory - I'd have hung around eating more even if they were pouring bear urine.

Passing the campground that was buzzing with the excitement caused by a nocturnal marauding bear, (I knew the feeling), I trekked northwards on the trail again, passing the Devil's Postpile and traversing pumice slopes and then the High Trail as I headed for my supply point of Tuolumne Meadows about fifty eight kilometres away. Before getting through though, I would have to climb to Donahue Pass at 11,056ft (3370m) which lay thirty five kilometres away on the boundaries of the Ansell Adams Wilderness and the Yosemite National Park.

I made about nineteen kilometres that day, and was on the move again the following morning at 0600. That was after fifteen minutes of leaping up and down with a long stick in my hands like a manic pole-vaulter.

The reason for my early morning callisthenics, was my bear-bag. The damn thing had somehow become entwined around itself during the night and dangled there just out of reach. I eventually managed to untangle it by running at it, leaping into the air and whacking the bag with a hefty length of broken branch.

I hoped there were no bears lurking in the undergrowth and taking notes.

There was no shortage of water on this stretch and besides creeks, the area was well endowed with lakes of varying size.

There was also a fair bit of snow around and when I reached icy Thousand Island Lake, the white panorama with its surrounding mountains was quite inspiring.

Incongruously, stuck in the snow was a small wooden signpost marked Donahue Pass!

Great! You don't see many of these signposts I thought. Now I know for sure where I'm going! I happily trudged off across the snow towards a gap in the range indicated by the sign.

It took about half an hour before vague feelings of doubt began to set in, then another half hour before I had *real* feelings of doubt and stopped, getting out my map and compass.

From memory, the range up ahead of me wasn't fitting the map contours.

I peered intently at my map. Nope! couldn't make that lot fit. I studied my compass. I'd been heading in a south westerly direction towards the Ritter Range. According to my map the trail should be leading in a north westerly direction *parallel* with the Ritter Range! Trustingly, I'd wandered off in the direction indicated by the sign.

Some cretinous dork must have moved it or else stuck it in the wrong place! I was headed towards Banner Peak/Glacier Pass!

I retreated back towards my starting point, a totally disgruntled blob with enough steam coming out of my ears to start melting snow. Damn! The mistake had cost me about two extra hours of walking. At least I was now back on course and paying *much* more attention.

I steamed over Island Pass at 10,200ft to eventually gain Donahue Pass, giving way to magnificent views of towering Mount Lyell, Yosemite's highest peak at 13,144ft, its northern wall enveloped by Lyell Glacier. The crossing of Island Pass was so easy as to be unnoticeable and the higher Donahue Pass was not that much more difficult. The tricky passes further south had set a good benchmark and had raised my apprehension threshold to a healthier level of confidence!

Four creek crossings and I had finally descended into the bottom of Lyell Canyon over 2000ft below, and was well and truly in Yosemite National Park.

The trail followed the western bank of the canyon river and I bowled merrily along enjoying its greeness, patched only occasionally by snow. I was not far from Tuolumne Meadows campgrounds now and even the southern end of the canyon is not much more than three hours hike from Highway 120, so I was beginning to see more and more day and weekend hikers about.

Fielding queries such as where I'd hiked from was a novelty at first, but the experience soon started to become a bit too repetitious and I ended up tending to avoid contact when I could. It would have been a good idea to print a card with all the relevant answers that I could just hold up for people to read -

1. Mexico, 2.Canada, 3. New Zealand, 4. Between 23-33 kilometres a day, 5. In a tent, 6. Dehydrated.

I pitched my tent in a small clearing about eight kilometres from Tuolumne, (I could almost smell the coffee!) re-fuelled with a pot of re-hydrated cajun chicken and rice, then wandered off to locate a suitable tree to string up my bear-bag.

All necessities taken care of, I circled my tent laying down the, "anti-bear urine circle" and crawled into my sleeping bag to drift off into dreams of tomorrow's culinary delights.

Rustle, Crash, Rustle!

I was instantly awake. I checked my watch, it was 0400.

The noise had momentarily stopped, but I thought I knew what it was. Deer tend to carefully make their way *around* undergrowth and tents, making little noise except maybe the quick nervous bursts of their hooves that you can pick up vibrating on the ground that you're lying on.

Your average macho bear on the other hand is not quite so subtle, and he tends to just push his way through the undergrowth with a sort of *gerrouttamygoddamway* kind of attitude.

Rustle, Pad, Pad, GROWL!!

Oh no! It *was* a freakin' bear!

I lay there with my heart doing a reasonably good impression of a defective Thompson sub-machine gun and clutching a suddenly pathetic looking Swiss Army knife (it works for McGyver so don't knock it!).

A nano-second after opening the massive two and a half inch blade, it occurred to me that it was going to be rather difficult disembowelling a frenzied bear with it and the only other alternative, would be a quick hari kari-like thrust into my own chest if the bear decided to join me in my tent.

I was totally miserable, neither scenarios appealed very much to me.

My unwelcome visitor now sounded very close-by.

I very slowly raised myself up from the prone position and peered out through the top of the tent door flap that I'd left slightly open for ventilation - Maybe I could get a photo' and impress the hell out of the folks back home.

Ventilation was the key word when I saw what was outside. The hairy guy was down on all fours, but even then he was *bigger* than my tent, and circling around about two metres away!

Pad, Pad, groan, GROWL, ROAR!

Stuff the nature watch and the impressive photographs!

I ducked back down into my sleeping-bag like a tortoise whipping its head back into its shell, and decided that my best plan was to assume the foetal position protecting my soft bits and hope that he'd piss off and find someone who smelt better.

He hung around my camp for at least ten minutes after that, and ten minutes is a *long, long* time when you're being monstered by a bear. If there are any adrenalin freaks reading this, then this is what you've got to do - try lying on the ground about 2m away from a 250kg bear that is roaring its bloody head off - trust me, you will not get a bigger buzz!

Thankfully, his shuffling and growling eventually faded to silence and he disappeared, only to be followed minutes later by a series of rending crashes and tearing noises from the direction in which I'd hung up my bear-bag.

Oh shit! There go my goodies. At least I wasn't featuring on the menu and looking on the bright side, I was so glad that I hadn't lapsed from my nightly ritual of removing the aromatics from the tent.

The sounds of ripping, crashing and tearing eventually stopped, and I drifted in and out of sleep for the next hour or so before cautiously getting up and wandering off to assess the damage.

The branch that my bag had been suspended from now lay on the ground, ripped from the tree by my nocturnal visitors. The line was tangled around the branch with a shredded bag at the end of it. All that remained of my food was the odd tattered empty packet.

The only thing that hadn't been completely devoured was a tube of toothpaste. Someone had taken a bite at it and decided that they didn't like the flavour. I considered this and decided that I might be on to something, I'd just need a test pilot to try out my McLean's Mint, Bear Repellant Spray.

There was even an impressive dent in my alloy fuel bottle that I'd left in the bag. Luckily it hadn't interested them enough to have a go at puncturing it. Though they had pierced a water bottle that I'd left under the tree.

I gathered up my stuff and headed off for Tuolumne, thankful that my food hadn't been walloped by these bandits a few days earlier.

There should be a re-supply parcel waiting for me there, plus I knew there was a store where I could add a few extras to make up for the loss.

Tuolumne Meadows was a hive of activity, with plenty of sightseers passing through.

They had quite a substantial store and diner set up, along with a small postal agency adjacent to the store. The structures were semi-permanent, being taken down before the onslaught of winter.

"Why's that?", I asked.

"'Cause there's about forty foot of snow in this spot come winter!"

Good reason, though it was hard to visualize that much snow with the hubbub of vehicles and people milling around in the bright sunshine at that moment.

I enquired at the post office to see if my parcel was there.

"Not here yet, probably be brought in from Yosemite village tomorrow."

I sloped off to join the queue at the diner and top up my flagging cholesterol levels.

That evening I pitched my tent on a grass verge not far from the complex, and surfaced the next morning just in time to see Vern, Ziggy and The Gimp arriving. We swapped a few trail stories and spent the morning just generally kicked back and trying to build up some decent fat reserves.

Ziggy was looking desperately thin, his knees were standing out like tennis balls suspended on strings.

Before starting his journey, Ziggy had thought that by the time he had finished it he would have thighs like The Incredible Hulk.

It looked like he was going to have to bulk up a tad before he was capable of even keeping his trousers *up*, let alone burst out of them as television's Incredible Hulk was apt to do.

He looked dismayed, "Man!, I've got to put on some weight, I think my body is starting to feed off itself."

He wasn't kidding. I wasn't faring much better myself, and I got a shock when I got a look in a mirror when I took a shower - I reminded myself of one of those pictures of a starved POW.

It was a bit of a worry.

The day was passing, and I decided to check in again with the post office to see what the parcel situation was.

"'fraid there's nothing come in from Yosemite today. Could be there, but they might not get it out for a couple of days."

"Damn." I couldn't afford to wait around for a couple of days on the chance that it *might* come in. I needed the food, and more importantly, I needed the next lot of trail maps and replacement boot inserts that would have been in the parcel.

The two Wilderness Press books that detailed the crest trail and contained the necessary maps were too heavy to carry in their entirety, so what I had done was to rip out the various sections and then have them forwarded on to me at intervals along with my supply parcels.

I decided to try and hitch into Yosemite village and see if they were there.

I went back to Ziggy, told him what I was going to do and he offered to keep an eye on my pack while I was gone.

"As long as you're back by tonight, we might get going again this evening or first thing tomorrow morning."

I took off down the road to try my luck hitching, or to see if there was a bus service of some sort.

For two hours I stood at the side of the road, thumb out like a dishevelled artist sizing up the distant mountains and watching vehicles speed by me with no sign of stopping. What's *wrong* with me?!

I spotted a woman walking my way with a couple of dogs in tether and crossed the road to ask her if there was a bus service of any kind into town.

She seemed quite relaxed, but her dogs started growling.

"Excuse me, could you tell me if there's a bus or anything that goes into town from here?"

"No, there's no bus service this way. Your only chance is to try and get a lift."

I looked exasperated, "I've been trying for two hours, but no one seems to want to stop."

"Yeah", she replied, " it could be a problem, folk are a bit wary nowadays to pick up strangers."

She looked at me for a moment, then added, "It could be your jacket...or your hat...or maybe your beard."

I suddenly remembered the suspicious reception that I'd received from the Inyokern police.

What she probably meant was, "It's hard for bums to get lifts."

That was it! I'd made the mistake of not hauling my pack with me.

Without it, I was transformed from being a clean living backpacking outdoor type, into a middle-aged derelict, probably ravaged by drugs and undoubtedly concealing a weapon in my jacket.

I thanked her for the advice, took off my hat and looked at my watch. Even if I got a lift now, it would be touch and go whether I got there before the post office closed for the day. I was just about to give up, when a van stopped.

"Where you headed?"

"I'm trying to reach Yosemite Village to pick up a supply parcel, but

I'm running out of time."

"Hop in, I can get you to the intersection of the main road that will get you into Yosemite. You'll get another lift easy from there."

I got in beside the driver, a tall thin guy in his early thirties wearing glasses and a martial arts T shirt, and we took off.

I was beginning to feel that now I might *just* make it in time. That was until he decided to modify the route slightly and insisted that, "As we're passing by the place, you just gotta see the giant redwoods!"

There was a signposted entrance to the area and despite my protests, he happily turned off down it, "Don't worry, you've got plenty of time to get to Yosemite Village!"

I couldn't figure out whether the guy was a well meaning moron, or just wouldn't listen. Simple mathematics said that if we fritzed around I wasn't going to make it in time before the post office closed. I still had to get *another* lift after this one just to reach Yosemite, and then try and hitch back again in time to let Ziggy get away.

I explained all this but the guy was in Redwood Spotting mode and just wouldn't listen. He parked the van and we walked down the pathway to the viewing area.

"Lookit that! That tree's so wide you could drive a bus through it!"

He was right, and the tree was impressive, but right then, rather than drive a bus through the tree, I felt more like driving his damn head through it.

"Yeah, good one, but I'm running out of time mate!"

I led back to the van in agitated silence. I didn't want to appear ungrateful, but the guy knew the situation and was screwing me around.

We eventually got to the intersection of the road leading to Yosemite and I got out with a terse thanks. He turned into the intersection heading in the opposite direction, and immediately stopped to pick up another hitcher.

Maybe it was the only way the guy could find people to talk to him.

I looked at my watch, it was too late to reach Yosemite on time by foot and unless I got another lift within the next ten minutes it was pointless going in as I had to return to Tuolumne that evening and couldn't stop over.

Two vehicles passed in the following fifteen minutes and neither stopped.

Cursing the bespectacled tree spotter, I fumed off down the road, returning in the direction of Tuolumne. Twenty minutes later, a car stopped and a father and son gave me a lift all the way back to Tuolumne.

Vern pulled out that evening, and Ziggy and The Gimp followed the next morning. I hung around till midday deciding what to do.

In the end, I discovered that the store sold copies of the California section of the Wilderness Press book. Using my plastic, I bought another copy of the book and loaded up with assorted junk and canned food that would see me through to the next supply point.

All that remained now was to mail home a roll of exposed film, then hit the trail north.

No problem. Wrong!

The young lady behind the mail counter of the store looked impassively at me.

"We only accept letters on a Sunday, no parcels."

Alarm bells rang. This young lady was definitely a trainee bureaucrat.

I gave her my most beguiling and servile look, "But I'm hiking out of here right now and won't be here on Monday."

"We only accept letters on Sunday."

"But the parcel is only the size of a roll of film, it almost qualifies as a fat letter!"

"We only accept letters on Sunday."

Her brain was stuck. I understood that some bureaucrats had that problem, so I tried to help her.

"Well, how about I give you the money for the postage now, you put the, "parcel" on a shelf, and then process it first thing tomorrow morning?"

"We only accept letters on Sunday."

I was beginning to lose it, which is a fatal mistake when dealing with bureaucrats, *"Look*, I'm trying to reach Canada before it snows, I can't wait around camped outside your little office waiting for the right time of month to hand over a bloody roll of film. Why can't you take my parcel and my money, and then when the moon is in the right phase and there's a goddam R in the month or whatever else it takes, *process the bloody thing?!"*

"We only accept letters on Sunday."

There was now a set look about her mouth, and she was looking at me as if I'd sinned against her and her entire family.

"This is unbelievable, I'm going to find someone with a brain!"

I stormed off and found the store manager.

I explained the situation to him and he was totally apologetic.

"Sorry about that, that's ridiculous, she's new on the job. Just give me the package and I'll see that it goes through."

Before shouldering my pack, I watched as he instructed the employee from hell to process my, "parcel".

She glared at me with more venom than any of the rattlers I was likely to meet.

Unfortunately, my victory didn't stand the test of time, as that particular roll of film never did turn up again.

I could be charitable and say that I thought it must have innocently gone astray in the system, but I'm inclined to think that a certain irate female postal clerk did a Jesse James on it.

May a thousand fleas infest her pants and, "Bad Hair" days plague her for the rest of her life!

My next supply point was at Little Norway about 240kms off. It was a fair distance, but I was looking forward to some enjoyable hiking, as the passes that I would now have to climb to were all below the top timberline.

The downside was that I'd be passing through some pretty active bear country, and after my previous experiences, I was hoping that my food and I would be left alone.

I cranked up another degree of easterly declination on my compass, and after a couple of aborted false trails, managed to find the one I wanted and pushed on in a north westerly direction, passing Tuolumne Falls and glad to be back in the woods again.

Just ten kilometres on I made camp for the night at Glen Aulin, taking advantage of a bear wire strung up high between two posts to hoist my food bag up out of harms way. I noted that both posts supporting the wire had been ravaged by bear claws at some time. Maybe the bastards had learnt to tightrope walk.

I had visions of a bear in a tutu, nonchalantly whistling as he looked the other way whilst cunningly inching his way along the wire towards my tucker!

I met Jeff (a Richard Widmark lookalike) and Alan here, a couple of teachers from San Diego. They kindly spent some time trying to locate some wild onions to show me what to look for if I wanted to supplement my dehydrated fare with a bit of greenery.

Unfortunately their search was unsuccessful and I completed my walk onionless, which in retrospect may not have been a bad thing - the combination of Louisianna beans and wild onions could have seen me farting my way north like a defective rocket.

Jeff was a great advocate for the bear. I found that out when I'd voiced my displeasure with the creatures, and suggested that it would be a good idea to have an open season on them once in a while to teach them to give humans a wider berth.

He was totally opposed to that, making the point that it was their territory and that we were the intruders. He pointed out that the grizzly was already decimated, and we'd end up with no bears at all if we weren't careful.

In retrospect, I now agree with him. The words of one old character that I'd met further south summed things up quite well I thought. We'd been talking about the various creatures in the area, and he'd drawled, "I kinda like the bears and rattlers. They give yuh somethin' to respect out here."

There was no denying that, they certainly commanded my respect, and definitely added a healthy helping of spice to the pudding.

It wasn't until later on in my journey that I felt I'd amassed sufficient retaliatory power to cope with any marauding bears.

The reason was a small stick of explosive that I'd found to the side of the trail, and from that night on my last move before drifting off to sleep was to carefully place the explosive beside me, securing my lighter to it with an elastic band. (for rapid deployment).

The cunning plan was, if any bear advanced beyond the, "Amazing Urine Circle", I would ignite the stick and hurl it out the tent, hopefully impressing the bear with my ability to make huge noises.

In retrospect, it was probably a good thing that the, "Amazing Urine Circle" was never broached.

I still have visions of the explosive missing the tent opening, bouncing back in on me and leaving me in a singed and demolished condition like the hapless Coyote in a Roadrunner cartoon.

After a spiceless night, I called out my farewells to Jeff and Alan, and by 0600 was heading north again along the banks of Cold Canyon creek. The trail was easy and pleasant going and I was making good mileage despite an earlier brief interlude of, "firefighting".

I'd spotted a steady curl of smoke rising lazily up from the undergrowth off to my side and made the slight detour to investigate.

Some moron had been camped there the night before, and had left the area with his campfire still smouldering. A breeze had fanned the embers and the rekindled flames were crawling through the ground cover towards some heavier growth and a stand of pines.

A little devil on my shoulder tried to persuade me that I shouldn't waste the time and energy doing anything about it, I'd be well out of the area before it could become a threat to me, and it wasn't my problem anyhow.

However, I'd been conditioned by twenty-odd years of dealing to this particular element, and my conscience wouldn't accept any excuses. So after kicking the little devil into touch, and leaping up and down on the incipient forest fire, I made several sweaty return trips down to the Cold Canyon creek to fill water bottles and douse the smouldering remnants.

I consoled myself with the thought that I'd surely score some karma points by doing such good works.

Several miles further on, my karmic reward for saving the continent of north America from a fiery ending, was to cross Return Creek and then make the stupid mistake of heading northeast into Virginia Canyon instead of southwest. This added thirteen unnecessary kilometres to my day and transformed me into a karmaless disgruntled blob that grumbled its way back the way it had come.

I hate it when that happens.

I spent the night on the western banks of Miller lake. There was supposedly an abundance of bears in this neck of the woods and I noted rather unhappily, that the trees in the neighbourhood didn't look like they were going to provide much in the way of a gantry for my bag of food. I didn't want to run the risk of losing my supplies again at this point, as I still had at least another eight days walking before I could re-supply. So against all recommendations, I decided to sleep with my food, which when you think about it, was rather Freudian.

I took the precaution of sealing my supply with a triple layer of three plastic bin bags, and then festooned the lot with my aromatic socks that

I hammered into shape around the outside of the bags. This was guaranteed to mask the smell of anything from a rancid vindaloo to a cooking haggis. My only vague doubt, was that if the local bears liked gorgonzola cheese, then I was in big trouble.

I performed the usual urinary circuit around my tent and retired for the night. It must have worked, as I surfaced unmolested the next morning.

The only creatures that were to cause me any lack of sleep for the next couple of nights were deer - The vibration of their footfalls would awaken me, as Rudolph the Yellow Nosed reindeer and his mates munched their way around my anti-bear urine circle.

I think they must have liked the salt content, because they would take practically no heed at all of my yelling and would brazenly retreat only a few steps before closing in again for their nocturnal snack.

I wouldn't have minded, but I only had a bladder big enough for one round of bear repellant, and the buggers were wiping it out.

I switchbacked down to ford the creek that ran through Matterhorn canyon, followed the canyon southwest for about a mile, then began the steep ascent up to Wilson Creek canyon before heading southwest up to windy Benson Pass. Next came Smedberg Lake, Piute Creek and eventually the climb to 9150ft Seavey Pass.

I'd bi-passed Benson Lake, resisting the temptation to detour to the southwest and visit its northern shore. This is described as the, "Benson Riviera", a long sandy beach that is formed when the lake's levels fall in mid or late season.

I'd pondered the side trip at the time and the incongruous sight of a beach in these surroundings would have been a novelty, but as I was enjoying the sandless scenery too much, and as I came from a region that was littered with beaches, I gave it a miss - another reason for foregoing the pleasure of building sandcastles, was the threat of mosquitoes, and Benson Lake looked like prime mossie country to me.

The mosquitoes in the Yosemite area were formidable.

They got in your eyes, in your mouth, and attacked any other exposed bits that protruded or dangled from your clothing.

At that stage I didn't have any repellent, and the damn things were fitted with bayonets which they continuously thrust into you.

They were the ultimate torture - death by a million bites, and the casual observer would have given me the wide berth deserving of a madman, as I advanced on him yelling abuse at an invisible enemy, arms whirling like propeller blades and hitting myself non-stop as I staggered along praying for a breeze that would stop the tiny tormentors from coming in for a landing.

At one stage I'd even become desperate enough to try to outrun them, rapidly wilting under the weight of my pack and eventually collapsing in a sweating heap and a cloud of mossies, who were by now whipped into a frenzy by the, "gravy" that was pouring from their reluctant dinner.

The little sods could even bite through cotton or polypropylene clothing, and I'd spent the end of one long tiring day forced to wear full wet weather gear under a clear sky and temperature of twenty-eight degrees celsius, struggling to make camp before dying of heat exhaustion.

My desperate mind had scoured the dusty recesses of my brain looking for a solution to the problem, but the best it could come up with was a dim recollection of having read somewhere that where you get dragonflies you don't get a problem, as mossies are, "piece de resistance" on the dragonfly menu. I vowed that the next time I sighted a dragonfly, I'd lasso it with a length of cotton and tether it to my backpack. I held dragonflies in new regard and whenever I spotted one hovering nearby, I looked on it with all the warmth that a ground trooper would reserve for an allied helicopter gunship.

Ants were another painful problem - being ungentlemanly enough to attack the family jewels whenever these valuable assets touched ground level. These ants were nothing like the small New Zealand species that you have to practically tap on the shoulder to get their attention. These fellows were big and very aware. You could just about see their eyes following your hand as it approached them, before they'd take off with a rapid change of course just as you attempted to zap them. They seemed to have perfected a cunning gameplan, whereby a couple of them would, 'run interference' whilst the remainder of the team would attack your soft bits.

If it was a choice between bears and rattlesnakes, or mossies and ants, then I'd go for the rattling and hairy ones any day.

Despite the insect nuisance, places like Kings Canyon and Yosemite were idyllic. The wildlife was everywhere and comparatively fearless. Deer were plentiful, and the total solitude and the beauty of the surroundings brought a lump to my throat.

If I'd been a poet I'd have composed a profound and beautiful ode to the moment, but the best I could manage was this pathetic limerick...

There was a young hiker named George
Who wandered with awe through the gorge
But the beauty soon palls, when an ant bites your balls
And through clouds of mossies you forge.

Leaving Yosemite after a thankfully windy and mosquitoeless camp on the banks of Dorothy Lake, the trail entered the Toiyabe National Forest where it remained, apart from occasional dips into the Emigrant Wilderness, before entering Carson-Iceberg Wilderness about six kilometres after Sonora Pass.

Sonora Pass was one of the few that you actually dropped down to. In this case a drop of some twelve hundred feet that took me down to 9620ft.(2932m). The terrain had begun to change markedly now, its origins being mainly volcanic and some high exposed alpine-like traverses of ridges were made before the final descent to Sonora Pass that was intersected by highway 108.

The barren and stark snow covered volcanic rock gave me a slight feeling of vulnerability, and I was quietly relieved to begin the descent. The area seemed so isolated that I was surprised to meet up with another hiker an hour or so before the pass.

Paul Churchill was a chef, out enjoying a day hike. He kindly presented me with a peanut butter sandwich, which after a diet of dehydrated food, was the equivalent of nectar, and worthy of preparation by none less than a chef. Paul accompanied me to the pass where he'd left his vehicle, giving me a lift down the road to bottle some water from a spring that he knew of, before returning me to the trail.

I was grateful for this, as it was nearing the end of my day and I was down to a few mouthfuls. The alternative of melting snow would have proved a tedious and fuel consuming exercise.

I added yet another American to my, "Here's my address, if you're ever in Auckland and need somewhere to stay" list, waved farewell and disappeared to some level ground just above the road to set up camp for the night.

It occurred to me that by the end of my journey, if every American visitor to NZ took me up on my offer, I'd be just about establishing a fifty first state in Auckland.

It was hard not to hand out the invitations though. I think the isolation and "hardships" of this journey made even the smallest kindness take on a depth of appreciation that would be non existent in everyday life. The invitations were about the only way I could think of for showing my appreciation.

From here I had another 119kms before I reached Little Norway near highway 50, and then only another two and a half kilometres to get to the Echo Lake resort post office and my supply parcel.

Homing northwards again, I picked my way through snow patches, crossed the 10,500ft saddle below Sonora Peak and traversed above the western side of Wolf Creek Lake. The trail reached a windy saddle at

10,250ft where it then entered the Carson-Iceberg Wilderness and dropped steeply past weatherbeaten whitebark pines and ice-shattered boulders to eventually parallel the Carson River.

The drop from this saddle was a bit of a milestone, and one of the psychological pluses that occurred every now and then. The reason being, that for the next 2655kms of trail between here and Canada, I would never again climb above the 10,000ft (3038m) mark.

I'd now walked for over one 1600kms, my legs and morale were holding out, and I was beginning to get the feeling that barring accidents I was going to make it!

Talking of accidents, the name Carson-Iceberg Wilderness intrigued me.

Who named it that? There was certainly a bit of snow and ice around, but *icebergs!*

I plodded along, mentally posting an extra man in the crowsnest on lookout duties.

The captain of the Titanic had thumbed his nose at icebergs, and I wasn't going to fall into the same trap.

Headlines of, "Foreigner Sunk By Rogue Iceberg Whilst Fording Carson River!!" and, "Foreigner's Tent Collides With Iceberg In Early Hours Of Morning!!" played around in my head.

Maybe there were bloody *Polar Bears* in this neck of the woods!

Maybe I'd *overshot* and gone too far north or something!

This was all good stuff, and it helped relieve the boredom of, "pickin' 'em up and puttin' 'em down."

Successfully navigating the iceberg wilderness without recourse to the lifeboats, I entered its neighbour the Mokelumne Wilderness at Raymond Meadows. My intended camp site that night was the relatively contour-line-free Upper Sunset Lake, just north of Indian Valley.

On reaching the boundary of Mokelumne I had a clever idea.

After reading the comments in my trail guide, together with a bit of map study, I was aware that if I left the PC trail and took off on compass bearings I could probably knock about nine kilometres off the distance that the designated trail took to reach Sunset Lake.

I was about to set off on a selected westerly bearing, when a quick last minute scan of the guide book caught the words, "false readings". I didn't like the sound of that and read on. Apparently just north from there, between the Wet Meadows and the Blue Lakes areas, for a distance of about ten or eleven kilometres, there were awkward things like magnetic anomalies, where a compass is apt to enter the twilight zone.

Remembering Hoyles' Law which states, "That which may possibly go wrong will go wrong", I deduced that the anomalies would probably extend southward through my intended course causing all sorts of mayhem, and immediately canned the idea of a shortcut. Which in the end was just as well, as the designated trail led me through some impressively rugged country that was worth the extra mileage.

0550 and I was on the trail again, Sunset Lake slowly falling behind me as I studied my maps once more, relishing the names of the next three locations ahead,
Border Ruffian Flat...The Nipple...Lost Lakes.
What more could I ask, it was all there, Violence, Sex, and Mystery!

It was not long after Lost Lakes that I met up with Matthew.
He had started his hike a couple of hundred kilometres south, and like me his next stop was Little Norway. He was going to rendezvous with his girlfriend there, and together they intended carrying on to Canada. I liked Matthew, he was cool. He had a friendly laid back nature, looked competently trail worn, carried only the necessary basics, and was completely designer-label free.
He entertained me with tales of life in Mexico, where he'd spent some time living with his girlfriend, as well as giving me some insights into the life of the American Indians of whom he had an interest. We even

managed to delve into the Gaia hypothesis of messrs Lovelock and Margulis.

All this was pretty heady stuff after days of riveting entertainment that consisted of nothing more stimulating than grunting to myself, conversing with marmots, and making up limericks about hikers from down under!

Crossing Carson Pass, we camped later that day above the Upper Truckee River, sheltered under mountain hemlocks and lodgepole pines and the following morning covering the eleven or so kilometres to emerge at Little Norway on Highway 50.

Carson Pass was christened for the history books in the winter of 1844. It was then that, "The Pathfinder", John C. Fremont, leading a government financed expedition headed into the range from the east with the famous mountain men, Kit Carson and Tom, "Broken Hand" Fitzpatrick. (Love those names!).

The thirty five year old Carson had been acting as a guide for the expedition, a role he was probably well suited for, as for fifteen years, he'd previously made his living as a trapper and fur trader after running away from his Missouri home at the age of fifteen.

The trio had been warned by local Indians that they would meet, "Rock upon rock - rock upon rock - snow upon snow - snow upon snow", and that even if they managed to get over the snow, they would not be able to get down from the mountain. Unheeding, they had obstinately pushed on, suffering hunger and snow blindness, until on February 6th, they reached a peak from which they could see the Sacramento Valley. Eight days later they reached the Sierra Crest at a point near Carson Pass, before eventually making a successful but difficult descent.

I've a suspicion that I'm a bit of a fair weather adventurer and would have tended to wait for the start of summer before heading into the mountains - or else gone home and eaten my sandwiches there when it started to snow.

I guess that's why there's unlikely to ever be a Spearing Pass!

Echo Lake, my supply point, was about another two and a half kilometres further on from Little Norway , but this was as far as Matt and I got.

The reason was a small bar/cafe at the side of the road. This was too good to pass by and we piled inside.

It proved to be a good call. The beer and food was excellent, I caught up on the latest episode of, "The Simpsons", and John the Mexican barman let us use his quarters to get showered up. We were also kindly given permission to put up our tents for the night on the vacant patch at the rear of the bar.

John was a bit of a character and if he was to be believed, had spent some time as a Smoke Jumper, in between training in karate alongside Elvis Presley.

Smoke Jumping is a kind of double jeopardy.

They throw you out of an aircraft to parachute in and fight fires in remote locations. The money's not bad, but that only reflects the risks that you take to earn it.

I'd done a bit of parachuting and a bit of firefighting, but hadn't got around to mixing the two - after hearing some of John's stories, I decided that I'd stick to jumping out at fires from nothing higher than the height of a truck cab.

Matthew's girlfriend arrived the next morning and after a pleasant day, I wished them well and headed on to Echo Lake, where I sorted out my supplies and mailed off my ice axe and a pair of sneakers that I'd never got round to wearing. I figured that as I was past the high snow country now and as it was July the second with the summer thaw well and truly under way, I wouldn't be needing the axe again. It could still have been useful as a digging tool and a climbing support, but the extra weight didn't warrant the effort.

I knew that barring accidents, my daily mileage should get me to Canada before the snows began in earnest again, so I took the chance and got rid of it.

I found out later, that Matthew and his girlfriend hadn't been so lucky.

After leaving Little Norway they had made less daily mileage than me and had been caught out by the onset of winter and heavy falls of snow. They'd had some hairy moments, and had been forced to bail out of the mountains before reaching the Canadian border.

To some people, my pre-occupation with gaining mileage must have seemed obsessive, but I knew that it was simply a question of mathematics. If I didn't put in the miles then there was no way I was going to get there in time. Although Matt didn't fall into the category, I'd already met up with a few dreamers on the trail, who I just *knew* weren't going to make it. They'd either be dangerously under equipped, or else they'd be swanning around doing thirteen or fourteen kilometres a day and hoping for a long summer.

I could think of nothing worse than putting in months of effort to achieve a goal, only to be beaten by the weather at the eleventh hour.

Looking at my map, I could see that water was going to be no problem at all in the next segment, which was the Desolation Wilderness area of the Eldorado Forest.

The map looked like it had been hit with a shotgun using lakes as pellets. The glaciers that had dug out these lakes had been around until about 10,000 years ago, which I suspect geophysically speaking, is just last week. The same glaciers had also dug out a lot of the existing soil, with the result that there were a great deal less trees in this particular area - hence the name Desolation.

This lack of forestation proved to be fairly handy for me, as it made cross country travel on compass bearing a lot easier. I had to do this, because in thoroughly unCrockett-like manner, I took a wrong turning and ended up on the wrong side of appropriately named Lost Corner Mountain.

This 8261ft lump on the ground provided a fairly substantial clue that I'd gone wrong, when it loomed up on my left hand side instead of my right.

I suspect that had I been wandering around these areas 150 years ago, rather than ending up with a cool nickname like Pathfinder Fremont, I'd have ended up with something a bit less inspiring, like, Wrong-Way Spearing...

George, Mountain Goat Vern and The Gimp, getting in a bit of R&R at Tuolumne Meadows

Chapter Seven

The Lovely Carola, Shasta-Trinity, The king of snakes, Milt, and

Sierra City.

My next supply was the small town of Sierra City, about 160kms and five days away.

The five days passed uneventfully, leaving me to slowly make my way north, adding more locations to an already substantial wake... Barker Pass...fording the headwaters of Whiskey Creek, American River and Squaw Creek...traversing the slopes of Anderson Peak...Donner Pass...Castle Pass, and then taking advantage of the well constructed Peter Grubb hut to spend a night without having to pitch a tent.

Just before reaching the hut, I'd once more met up with Ziggy and The Gimp as they made their way through Castle Valley, and the three of us spent the night enjoying the hut's comparative luxury.

"Enjoying" was probably the wrong word as far as Ziggy was concerned.

He'd been having a few stomach problems and spent most of his time perched unhappily in the unusual two-storey detached long drop. His slow climb to the perch was quite hazardous, as any sudden or unusual contortions would result in disastrous explosions from his nether regions.

His pale suffering bespectacled head, crowned with a Noddy-like cap, would emerge from atop the long drop, accompanied by depressed moans and groans of complete misery.

His demeanour couldn't have been helped by the comments and shrieks of laughter that this produced from The Gimp and I.

Joking aside, we understood his concern, as the spectre of giardia was never far from our minds.

Luckily for Ziggy, the attack turned out to be a forty-eight hour wonder and his rapidly accelerating weight loss was arrested just before he vanished into the mountain air.

There's a fantastic amount of comparatively recent history in these regions, and travelling through them gave me an inkling as to the hardships that the early American settlers must have endured.

Many of them, either unwittingly or by force of circumstances had traversed these areas in the winter months without the comfort of, "Hi-tech" gear, medications or adequate food supply. When you add to this the continual threat of harassment by local Indians, who might at any time attack them or their livestock, then you realize that they must have been either a very naive or a very determined bunch.

Donner Pass was named after George and Jacob Donner, the leaders of 82 men, women and children in 23 wagons, who, because of various errors and misfortunes, reached the Sierra Nevada in October 1846 after winter had set in.

Floundering in snow, and hopelessly trying to get themselves and their wagons through the Pass, their food supplies had dwindled away to nothing. They made crude shelters on the shores of a frozen lake below the pass, then on December 16th, a group of 17 men and women set out with 6 days rations, heading for the settlement of Bear Valley.

More than a month later, 7 emaciated members of the party, which included all 5 women, arrived at an Indian village.

They'd survived by eating their dead comrades.

A rescue party reached the others on February 18th and found a starving group of 47, surviving by boiling cattle hides and bones for hours, and then, as a member died, they ate him.

The horrors of that journey must have left some pretty deep physical and emotional scars on the survivors, who no doubt had to pick up their lives and get on with it without any of today's therapeutic counselling.

The last surviving member of this ill-fated party, Isabella Breen, died in 1935.

For anyone taking the severity of winter travel lightly, it's worth reading up on this incident. It's a sobering account of the strengths and weaknesses of the human spirit.

We left the hut at 0615 the following morning, and after thirty five kilometres made camp at Jackson Meadow Reservoir, eighteen kilometres from Sierra City.

There was a campground here with a few facilities and we eyed them greedily.

Problem was, there was a fee to be paid for the privilege, and although we had the money, it went against the grain to suddenly have to pay to put your tent up after months of living in the woods rent free.

We discussed this, and it was decided that as I was the The Foreigner, I should approach the camp guards and see if we could pitch our tents *gratis* within the camp boundaries.

The rationale being that they would be more receptive to a visitor from a distant clime who had walked so far.

The one snag with this plan, was that I am notoriously inept at asking for favours and the request for free ground space went something like this,

"G'day. How much does it cost to camp here for the night?"

"X dollars."

"O.K. Thanks."

Ziggy and The Gimp expectantly awaited my return.

"What'd they say?"

"It's no good, we'd have to pay."

That idea was immediately vetoed, and we slunk back into the woods to enjoy a Scotsmans' campground. We didn't need a shower anyway, it wasn't even August yet.

Sierra City was a pleasant stopover, though the American concept of a city must be radically different to that of a Kiwi's or a Brit's, as this city consisted of not a great deal more than a general store, a bar, a couple of other small stores and an eating house or two.

I think it must have owed its livelihood to a combination of commuters living there, campers visiting there, and maybe some trade from the mines surrounding it.

Looking at my map, I could see a variety of evocatively named mines sprinkled around the area...Klondyke...Sierra Buttes...Phoenix...Sacred Mound...Kentuck...Dottie Q.

I half expected to find that old fortyniner Gabby Hayes getting a grubstake at the general store.

I'd by now discovered that in some of these small trailside communities, there are kindly people that make a point of supplying hospitality to each year's wave of Pacific Crest trail hikers. This was a nice touch of humanity and generally a welcome phenomena, but some of these folk could become a bit insistent as it were, and you could end up feeling as if you were being, "collected" as part of a hobby rather than being given the assistance that you may want.

Ziggy, The Gimp and I, had been joined outside the general store by a couple of other hikers who were in the area doing a section of the trail.

It wasn't long before Sierra City's local benefactor zeroed in on us and started herding us in the direction of his house, where he seemed to be taking it for granted that we would pitch our tents in his back garden. Now, he was probably a genuine sort of guy, but I just didn't feel like camping in his back yard like one of a set of garden gnomes or something.

There were five of us now and I just didn't want to be part of a group. I enjoy company, but only for spells that I can walk away from when I feel the need.

After all, that was really what my journey was all about.

I told him I thought I'd just wander to the edge of town and pitch my tent there.

A frown darkened his face, and he looked quickly at the others as if ready to quell any further sign of insurrection that my anti-social behaviour might precipitate.

He scowled at me and rapidly shepherded them away.

I retired the few hundred yards to the edge of town, and out of sight, made a peaceful camp in the trees above a steep wooded gully.

I mentioned my frame of mind to Ziggy the next morning as we took a beer in the bar.

He knew where I was coming from, and admitted that he too would rather have had a bit of solitude.

This was not entirely undue to the fact that Ziggy's stomach problem still hadn't cleared completely, and he bravely announced that he had made the decision to hitch a ride into the nearest large town and visit a doctor.

I expressed the hope that he didn't self-explode and send the vehicle careering off the road as the hapless driver let go the wheel and clawed at the windows in a desperate attempt for air.

I also took the opportunity of putting in a somewhat topic-related order for a pair of underpants - I only had two pairs for the journey, so they were getting some pretty heavy duty use and could do with a bit of relief. My mail parcel with some new boot inserts and some film wasn't due in until the following day, so I had some waiting time to spare.

Ziggy arrived back the next morning, complete with anti-giardia medication and my new underpants.

They were the shorts type, with little pictures of various types of fruit on them and very chic – the problem was they were approximately fifty-five sizes too big.

The next twenty minutes were spent entertaining Ziggy and The Gimp and testing the effectiveness of Ziggy's anti-explosive medication as I modelled the oversize shorts on the village green.

The legs of the underpants dangled down below the legs of my hiking shorts and it made me look like me Mum had dressed me funny.

The only answer seemed to be to wear my new, "Fruit of the Loom" underdaks *on top* of my hiking shorts.

This was bound to start a new craze and would fall nicely into line with the absurd fashion of wearing your running shorts outside your tracksuit pants.

I'd finished my impromptu modelling session, and we were sitting on the grass discussing our plans for the next leg of our journey.

A local pulled up outside the store opposite us, hopped out of his car and disappeared inside the store.

The road was sloping quite steeply where he'd stopped and it suddenly became apparent that he'd forgotten to apply his handbrake before getting out of the vehicle.

I watched mesmerized as the vehicle gained momentum, heading for the plate glass of a store on the opposite side of the road.

Not so The Gimp - he was up on his feet in a flash, sprinted across the road and jogging alongside the car managed to open the door and stamp on the brake.

It was an impressive display of quick thinking, and I could see that The Gimp was justifiably proud of his action when he explained the new location of the vehicle to its owner who eventually emerged from the store.

I watched for the reaction of the driver as The Gimp spoke to him - the thought had crossed my mind that maybe we'd all get a beer out of this!

The driver's reaction was zero.

He just got into his car and drove away.

The Gimp joined us again, "Didya see that! The ungrateful sucker didn't even say thanks!

I shoulda let his freakin' car trash the goddam town!"
We were in full agreement.

Ziggy and The Gimp had decided to stay on for another day, so after donating my new unsullied and uncomfortable undershorts to Ziggy, who would in his present condition no doubt find them a useful backup, I studied my map and that afternoon headed out of town.

I decided to take a shortcut. The map showed that to reach the PC trail, I would have over a mile of road walking to the east and then a steep switchbacking climb up along the trail before it swung back above itself and meandered off to the west.

I opted for another trail shown on the map that was much closer to town, cutting up between the Sacred Mound and Kentuck mines to intersect the PC trail after about a mile. This cut out about six kilometres and also eliminated the road walking that I disliked.

I managed to locate this alternate trail, and all went well until I rounded a bend to come up against a barrage of home made trespass notices.

There must have been seven or eight of them nailed around the trees...PRIVATE PROPERTY...NO ADMITTANCE...KEEP OUT...TURN BACK...etc.,etc.

As well as these unwelcoming signs, in the near distance I could hear what sounded like a couple of oversized hounds of the Baskervilles barking away like they were in the process of disembowelling some other unfortunate lover of the wilderness.

This development was disconcerting, the abundance of warning signs hinted at obsessive behaviour. I can tend to ignore official notices of command with a sort of, "me against the establishment" attitude. However, this smacked more of a situation requiring a, "me against the Psycho Raving Lunatic of the Woods" attitude.

This was not the sort of scenario that I had planned for myself and called for a rapid change of course, the hounds of the Baskervilles would soon be through with their current victim and would no doubt be sniffing me out at any minute.

I looked at my map, a steep and densely wooded ridge ran up to the PC trail off to my left. The sound of barking was drawing closer, so I rapidly disappeared into the foliage and began bushwhacking my way up the steep incline.

After about an hour of slow progress, snagging my pack continuously in the undergrowth, I came up against a vertical granite wall. Damn!

Detouring to the side would only drop me into more impassable rubbish, it looked like I'd have to either retrace my steps or spend the rest of the day crashing around on the ridge.

So much for bloody shortcuts!

On the way up, I'd passed by a water pipe that someone had at some stage fitted up to catch the water that was emerging from a spring in the steep ridge. The pipe snaked away disappearing into the undergrowth in the direction of the baying hounds.

A rock slip had at some stage partially dislodged the pipe from its mounting, with the result that it was only catching a trickle of what it should have been.

It was a hell of a job getting up to it, which would have accounted for its poor maintenance, so I decided to do the decent thing and fix it while I was there. This gave me the satisfaction of saving my detour from being totally wasted, it also occurred to me as I got the thing running, that it might even act as a bargaining point when the hounds were at my windpipe.

Forgive those that trespass against you, for they hath given you thy daily water!

As silently as possible, I returned to near my starting point and edged my way around above the trespass notices to join the forbidden trail.

The hounds were not in evidence now, and I rapidly made my way past what looked to be an old abandoned mine and eventually reached the sanctuary of the PC trail.

I found out later from The Gimp, that he and Ziggy had also had the same shortcut idea as me, and had also come up against the trespass signs. Only difference being, they were sprung by the, "Psycho Raving Lunatic Of The Woods" who threatened them with all kinds of mayhem and abuse and a warning that he'd let his dogs loose on them if they took a step further.

I hoped that Ziggy's medication had risen to the occasion and met the ultimate test, and was also secretly thankful for the silence of solitary travel that had probably enabled me to escape detection and complete my elongated shortcut!

The westerly winding trail was now easy and pleasant, skirting the southern slopes of the rugged Sierra Buttes and providing me with excellent views to the south.

Larger pines had for the moment thinned out to be replaced by a variety of shrubs with names like manzanita, huckleberry oak, tobacco brush and bitter cherry.

The identification of flora has always been one of my weak points, and if it wasn't for the trail guide I wouldn't have had a clue as to the greenery that surrounded me.

I'm woefully ignorant of all plant life and stand in awe of those who can stroll along, casually casting authoritative gems like, ".....and that specimen there of course, is a *vegitus obscurus* of the *namus forgetlia* family."

I vow one day to take an intensive course of David Bellamy pills, and then impress the hell out of my fellow peasants.

I had close to 160kms of trail before reaching the small resort of Belden near Highway 70, but only covered about thirteen of them that first day out of Sierra City, making camp just south of Tamarack Lakes. A couple of day hikers passed by my camp not long before sunset and seemed genuinely interested in the distance I'd covered so far.

Chuck and Joan Dahl were from Seattle, and kindly left me with some water, Gatorade, a nectarine and an invitation to call them collect when I eventually reached Snoqualmie Pass in Washington.

They suggested that if my schedule allowed it, they would pick me up from Snoqualmie and give me a day or two of showers and decent food at their home.

As it turned out, I didn't take them up on their generous offer, but I was touched by their kindness, and they played no small part in elevating both my spirits and the kudos of the American people.

The PC trail passes along the banks of many lakes and creeks on its course north, but because of its usual high elevation, it also passes *above* many others.

Gold Lake was one of those that I was able to gaze down upon.

This lakes' claim to fame, was that it was named in recognition of a hoax engineered by an English con man by the name of J.R. Stoddard.

One of the rumours of the gold rush days, was that somewhere in this vicinity there was a lake whose banks were strewn with gold for the taking. The wily con man had turned up in Nevada City with a small amount of gold, and a story that he had found the fabled lake whilst out on a hunting trip. Unfortunately, as he was scooping up the loot, he was attacked and wounded by Indians, and barely managed to escape with his life.

What he was willing to do he said, was to share his good fortune with whoever was in turn willing to pay him a fee to lead them back to the lake.

In the summer of 1850 he set off into the mountains with dozens of fee paying hopeful's, as well as a huge throng of, "freeloaders" tagging along in their footsteps.

This aspect of the incident really appealed to me - I had visions of hundreds of opportunists casually whistling and trying to look nonchalant and inconspicuous as they shuffled along behind the paying party, bumping into one and other everytime Stoddard and his party stopped.

"You're following us!"

"Oh, hullo! No we're not! Fancy seeing you here!"

The days went by with no sign of the lake, and the disillusioned prospectors began to get suspicious, muttering things about decorating one of the pine trees with a Stoddard wind-chime. This was Stoddies cue to make himself scarce, and he shot through during the night, leaving a goldless cast of hundreds to greet the dawn!

I continued my way along the trail, trending north westerly across the map, crossing and recrossing the invisible Plumas and Sierra county lines, skirting the volcanic cliff faces of Gibralter peak and Mount Etna, until eventually leaving the panoramic views provided from Bunker Hill Ridge and entering decidedly into Plumas county.

Twenty seven kilometres from here I thankfully made the long descent to camp alongside Middle Fork Feather River. My 38kms day had provided pleasant and scenic walking, but the temperatures had been up to 107 degrees and I needed watering inside and out.

As I approached the river, I noticed a couple of hikers at its edge, dwarfed by the large equestrian bridge that spans its banks. I was delighted to find that the two figures were Stefan and Carola, a German couple that I had met up with at different points along the way.

They were taking an extended holiday along the trail, making use of public transport to skip sections as they headed north, and then hike in to the more scenic parts.

At our last meeting, we'd shared a humorous moment when we were joined at our campsite by an American hiker whom we'd run into a week or so previously.

At that time he'd just acquired a, "tin whistle", and had informed us that he was going to teach himself to play as he wandered along the trail.

"How's the flute going?", I had asked.

"Not bad, I've come on quite a bit and I'm getting the hang of it now. I'll give you a bit of a tune."

We sat back in anticipation, expecting to be impressed with an Irish jig or two, or at worst a hesitant version of Three Blind Mice.

He seriously and studiously cleared his throat, put the instrument to his mouth and proceeded to give a faltering rendition of Doh...Ray...Me...Fah...Soh...Lah...Tee...Doh.

That was it! With a dexterity bordering on musical genius, he had in less than two weeks, self taught himself to lift one finger after another off the whistle to produce the musical scale!

What made it so funny was that he was genuinely pleased with his accomplishment, and when he had finished his performance, mistook the way we glanced at each other for looks of wonderment!

"Actually", he said, warming to the occasion and taking the chance to impress his audience even further, "I didn't find it too difficult to learn that."

He looked at us expectantly.

"Bugger me", I said, "You must be a natural"

Stefan made some humorous comment about Carnegie Hall, which thankfully allowed us to release some painfully suppressed sniggers and save the budding maestro from our philistine behaviour.

Stefan, who had attended college in America, had perfect American English with hardly a trace of German accent. His attractive partner Carola on the other hand, could speak only a little English, but her comely appearance and pleasant manner made up for any lack of verbal communication.

After catching up on latest events, the three of us decided that a cooling dip in the Feather river was in order, so I modestly stripped down to my underwear and approached the water.

Carola said something to Stefan and after a brief conversation in

German, began getting her gear off!...The Full Monty!...or rather in Carola's case...The Full Rommel!

Stefan turned smilingly to me, "She asked if it would be all right to take all her clothes off, and I told her of course, that is what hiking is all about!"

Yes! Yes! I couldn't agree more!

After months of gazing at nothing cuter than a well-groomed marmot, this was almost more than a man could bear!

I noticed Stefan slyly watching me for reaction, as the Naked Nordic Goddess cavorted in the water before me.

I of course being the gentleman that I am, thought of England and struggled desperately to appear blasé about the whole thing and to prevent my eyes from popping out like those eyeballs on the end of coiled springs that leap out at you from fake spectacles.

I stood there waist deep in the river, wishing that I was wearing my sunglasses, and with the water temperature around me rising dangerously.

To quote Charles Dickens from, "A Tale of Two Cities" (a title by the way, that *almost* sums up this situation!)

"It was the best of times, it was the worst of times!"

I was back on the trail again by 0545, and heeding the advice that Deadman Spring up ahead may now be dry, I filled my water bottles at the river, farewelled Stefan and Carola who were still happily ensconced in their tent and began chipping away at the remaining sixty kilometres to Belden.

After a long and very hot ascent to Bucks Summit, I entered the Bucks Lake Wilderness and spent the night camped just past Spanish Peak lying to the east of the trail, the following day making the twenty four kilometres and eventual steep descent down into Belden, meeting up again with a main branch of the Feather River that unfortunately no longer contained the lovely Carola.

I'd arrived at Belden at 1100, and seduced by the amenities and the store, spent the remainder of the day stuffing calories into myself and making use of the campground's shower facility.

I'd actually made camp outside the ground not far from the store, so technically I think that maybe I shouldn't have been using their shower, but no one challenged me so I went for it.

I found a small piece of soap that had been left by a previous visitor, dried myself off with my T shirt and emerged a new man.

Apart from a toothbrush and a small tube of toothpaste, I didn't carry any personal cleaning gear such as soap.

This was not so much a weight thing or even a dislike of washing. It was primarily because it didn't seem right to pollute the pristine waters of mountain creeks with a soapy scum.

Besides being some creatures' home, it was also the drinking water supply for anyone who happened to be out there.

Clean water was one of the things I'd learnt to appreciate from this trip and I was totally pissed off on one memorable occasion when my drinking water was suddenly transformed into a lavatory bowl by a group of horse riders.

I was crouched down at the edge of a lake filling my water bottles, when three riders appeared and walked their mounts knee deep into the water about ten metres away from me.

Of course the inevitable happened and the three horses took turns at emptying their bowels into the water, probably discharging a ton of giardia cysts in the process.

I couldn't believe it, the riders seemed totally unconcerned. Their horses could have easily drunk from the water without standing in it, or else been moved to a discreet distance from me.

I'd almost lost it and let them have both barrels, but I bit my tongue with the rationalization that I was the foreigner here and not the one to tell an American where he should park his horse.

I contented myself with an audible curse thrown in their direction, gave them the evil eye and grumped off muttering unhappily to myself.

I left Belden early the next morning, passing by an old two storey mining stamp mill. There was a weathered character leaning on the balcony and looking down at me from above - somehow he looked familiar.

"Hi George."

It was Mountain Goat Vern!

Vern hadn't been feeling too well, and was going to take a few days out of it.

Up close he didn't look too good, and I wondered to myself if maybe he had pushed himself too far.

He was going to find a doctor and get himself checked out. We wished each other well, and I carried on wondering if that was the last time old Vern would, "pop up".

My next supply was at Castella which was about ten hot days away, but I knew that four days from here I'd be able to take a slight detour and head for the diner at a place called Old Station. This diner of course was the carrot in front of the donkey and my stomach propelled me along with far more vigour than my leg muscles could ever manage. The other, "carrot" that dangled before me was the fact that I was now finally chipping away at the northernmost end of the Sierra Nevada Range and the next range, the Cascades, running the full length of Oregon and Washington, would take me all the way into Canada.

The easily followed trail wound its way in a westerly direction, running through the Plumas National Forest almost parallel with Chips Creek and passing by a small uninhabited log cabin and a harassed King snake.

The serpents' harassment was due to my focus being locked onto the log cabin that was nestled in an idyllic spot just thirty metres from the creek.

If it hadn't been for the snake's brightly banded colours, I would have stepped squarely on top of him instead of skidding to a halt and kicking him up the backside.

He was a handsome fellow about a metre long and quite slow moving. Because of this, I thought at the time that there must have been something wrong with him, but I found out later that this was his *modus operandi,* and he was quite capable of looking after himself.

He would even track a rattlesnake by its odour then kill and devour it...now that's got to be a ballsey snake!

Just the scent of one of these King snakes will put the poor maligned rattler into a defensive mode.

I hadn't imagined a rattler being too scared of anything, but as me old Mum used to say, "Every bug has a smaller bug upon his back to bite him!"

I played with the poor fellow for a while before losing interest and carrying on into the oppressive heat of the day.

The sultry weather eventually turned into an afternoon of thunderstorms that accompanied me most of the way to my camp at Cold Springs, 20kms from Belden. A large group of seventeen hikers from the Sierra Club were also camped in the area, and a bunch of them couldn't get over the fact that I'd only left Belden that morning. I in turn, couldn't get over the fact that they'd left Belden *three days ago!*

If the group had been around, they'd have been even further impressed, as the next two days saw me covering a distance of 74kms in 100 plus temperatures, to arrive at Warner Valley camp ground. This was close to my planned detour for Old Station and after crossing the flat layers of lava flow that made up Flatiron Ridge, I left the PC trail at Corral Meadows and took a combination of the Summit Lake trail, Highway 89, and Emigrant trail to eventually arrive at the Old Station diner.

After a substantial breakfast the following morning, I sat in the diner pouring coffee into myself and considering my next move.

I'd been told that there was a burnt out area on the Hat Creek Rim trail, as well as a desperate shortage of water on that route.

With the temperatures still clinging to the top end of the thermometer, I didn't feel like punishing myself for no particular reason and my thoughts turned to an alternative route.

I studied my maps and finally made the decision to take the more westerly Hat Creek trail and then take a day to road walk Highway 89 to the Burney Falls State Park.

From previous experience, I knew that although often quicker, road walking can be more wearying than cross-country.

The continuous pattern of foot-strike on a flat unyielding surface tends to aggravate my joints and if the road also happens to be busy, then the constant roar of traffic blasting past, gets right up my nose.

I considered this, but the road didn't appear to be particularly busy, it also offered the lure of a couple of small stores along the way and ran straight as a die towards my next objective.

That'll do me I thought, and set off.

I hadn't been travelling for long when the heat and the need to fill an empty water bottle forced me down off the road to a trickling creek that ran under it.

I slid rapidly down the bank and spun round under the abutment of the road, scaring the hell out of myself and the dishevelled character who was sitting there sheltering from the heat of the day.

We both took a step backwards and momentarily eyed each other, before mutually deciding that neither of us posed an immediate threat.

My new found acquaintance was called Charlie.

Charlie was a drifter.

Originally from Montana, he was heading nowhere in particular and living off odd-jobs and handouts. Local churches were good places to get both these he advised me. I t was hard to judge his age, he could have been anything from thirty to forty-five, but he seemed happy enough with his itinerant lot.

He eyed my water filter as I filled up a bottle from the almost stagnant creek that sported a couple of rusting cans and an empty Marlboro cigarette carton, "What's that?"

I told him it was a filter I used to make sure that I didn't get the trots from any contaminated water.

He moved to the edge of the creek, and with a swagger, scooped a handful of water into his mouth, "Hell, water don't scare me none!"

He sat down again and eyed me for effect.

I carried on pumping water through my wimpish filter, and decided that this called for a bit of rapid face-saving on my part.

" Well Charlie, I wouldn't normally bother with it, but I'm trying to walk all the way from Mexico to Canada and I can't take the risk of getting sick."

It was my turn to look for effect.

"You *walked* all the way here from Mexico?"

"Yeah."

"You mean you walked and *hitched a ride* now an' then."

"Nope. Walked *all* the way, through the mountains."

"Damn! I kin hardly believe that!"

"It's true."

"Damn!"

I could see that he was thinking about it, and was probably impressed enough to forgive me my wimpish behaviour with the water filter.

I got back onto the subject of how he survived from handouts, and mentioned that I'd seen some guys around San Francisco standing in the streets outside shopping malls and holding signs with the message, "I will work for food."

"Yeah, them guys don't want any work. They just hopin' someone'll give 'em some money. Hell, I've done that mahself. Sign keeps the police off your back!"

170

He paused and looked at me again, "You *really* walked all the way?"

"Yeah."

"Damn!"

We talked some more, and before leaving him to it, I asked him where he was headed.

He picked up his worn duffle bag and hung it over his shoulder, "Reckon I'll check out Chico, ain't never been there...."

Just before going our separate ways, I gave him a spare fish hook and a piece of the fishing line that I had. He seemed pleased with the gift, and responded with, "Thanks buddy, and good luck...You sure you didn't hitch *one* little ride?"

"Nope"

"Damn!"

***

As I'd thought, there wasn't much in the way of traffic along the road, apart from occasional logging rigs that would thunder past, sometimes empty, with their trailers piggy-backed on top of them. I guessed that they were probably headed through this part of the Lassen National Forest on their way to the timber in Washington or Oregon.

They were pretty big rigs hauling a fair old tonnage. I hoped that they were leaving some forest for me to walk through!

Although easy walking, the road was beginning to take its toll on my knee and I was glad to drop my pack at the door of a roadside store and wander inside out of the sun.

I was checking out the postcard stand in the corner of the small store when a local came in and started up a conversation with the owner who was watching me from behind the counter.

I was only half listening, when the word, "giardia" got my attention. I became even more focused when the owner loudly proclaimed,

"It's those Pacific Crest hikers that are causing it, crapping all over the place whenever they feel like it!"

171

I don't know whether the comment was made to wind me up or not, but my spring cranked several notches tighter.

There was one thing I'd seen from experience - All the long distance hikers I'd met out on the PC trail were almost paranoid about waste disposal.

They wouldn't even leave a sweet wrapper lying around, let alone a water-supply-threatening turd!

All the through hikers that I had met, myself included, took a pride in leaving no trace of where we'd been.

I couldn't contain myself and rounded on them, breaking into their conversation,

"Bullshit! I've just spent the last three months on that trail, and the ones that are causing giardia are the bloody day trippers and weekenders that drive up to the trail heads. They don't have to rely on creeks to drink out of and a lot of them don't give a stuff!

Think about it - would you crap in your own bloody water tank!!"

They both looked at me in stunned silence, and getting no response I grabbed my pack and steamed off down the road.

I'd mellowed out by the time I made my next close and pleasant encounter with one of the folk of Highway 89.

I was sitting on the ground, back up against the wall of the last general store I'd come across before reaching Burney Falls. I was studying my maps and trying to motivate myself for the next leg when an old car pulled up and three adults (Chinese American) got out and disappeared into the store.

"Hi!"

I looked up from my maps and saw two bright smiling eyes peering at me over the top of the car door, jammed in amongst several fishing rods.

The eyes belonged to a young Chinese girl aged about nine or ten.

"Hi, caught any fish?"

"No - but we're going to get some."

"Oh."

She kept smiling, "Where are you going to?"

"Canada, I've walked up from Mexico."

"Oh...Would you like an apple?"

She ran over and pressed four small apples into my hand, then shyly ran back to the car.

The adults returned, smiled and waved as they got back into the car and took off down the bumpy road.

The girl waved from the back window until they were out of sight.

The apples were sour....the touch of kindness made them sweet enough.

I hope life is good to her.

After spending the night camped in the woods at the side of the road, I finished off the remaining fourteen kilometres into the McArthur-Burney Falls Memorial State Park on the edge of the Shasta National Forest.

Nature was calling, so I joined the line of RV's and cars that were driving steadily into the park campground area, knowing that they'd have an ablution block where I could attend to business and clean up a bit.

Two female rangers were busy directing the incoming vehicles, whom I noted, were being charged a fee for the use of the campground. I waited until there was a break in the traffic and then approached the pair who were deep in discussion.

"Probably talking about the psycho hunter they faced down and 'cuffed before removing his AK47, or the rattler they took out in mid-strike with a shot from the hip", I thought.

As usual I was wrong of course.

They were actually discussing the attributes of their respective hairdressers.

It seemed a bit incongruous really. Two armed women extolling the virtues of a certain style of perm.

A bit like coming across Mike Tyson and Evander Holyfield discussing the merits of their favourite macrame stitch.

I waited until there was a lull in the conversation, and then smilingly turned on the old Spearing charm, "Well whoever did your hair certainly made a good job of it."

The armed amazon was obviously not impressed with my smooth talk and gave me a stoney look, "Can we help you sir?"

It sounded more of a threat that a request.

Oh oh, I thought, looks like my opening lines need a bit more practice - seemed to work okay with marmots.

"Hi, I'm hiking through on the PC trail heading for Canada, and I was wondering where I could camp."

Her face relaxed and broke into a smile, "Just find a spot in the campground, no charge for you guys. We figure if you can walk this far you get in for free. Don't move on without getting a look at the falls though!"

I found the ablution block, cleaned up, then sat down amidst the surrounding hubbub.

Cars, kids, radios and happy campers whirled around me. It was too much, I picked up my pack and headed for the trail again.

I took the ranger's advice, and before leaving, walked the parks' nature trail to check out the falls.

The 130ft falls was worth the small detour.

Considered as California's most voluminous, it dumps about 200 million US gallons a day. That's a puddle big enough to cover one square mile of land, one foot deep in water *every* day.

Reading my trail book, I found that it was fed from a massive subterranean reservoir which had the affect of keeping its volume constant, and its temperature at around forty-two degrees all year round

- very interesting. Standing there in the midday heat and considering my diminishing frame, I reckoned I could have done with the affects of some subterranean reservoir feeding myself.

Leaving the falls and paralleling Lake Britton, I climbed steadily up to a ridge some 600ft above the Pit River canyon before carrying on to cross Rock Creek and eventually reach Peavine Creek.

I made camp here for the night, as it had been a long tiring 23kms, making a total of 38kms for the day, but it was good to be alone again and away from the chaos and trappings of the park.

The only downer, was the discovery that the water supply had been polluted by the cattle that roam this area in the summer months. The next water along the trail was at Moosehead Creek, which was over 24kms away and out of the question.

Filter and iodine tablets were put to use and I crossed my fingers.

Since overhauling the filter a few days ago, I was a bit unsure if it was still sifting out the bugs. The thing had slowly become more and more blocked and discoloured, until filling a bottle had become a tediously slow process.

The actual filter was a sealed throw-away affair, but not having the luxury of a replacement, I had carefully broken its seal and washed the filtering material with safe water.

Judging by the colour of the material, my filter had become a high-density housing estate for millions of giardia lamblias.

Tampering with sealed units was probably not a good idea but I didn't have much choice, and monitored my potty habits with interest from then on.

I headed off again at 0600 the following morning, passing through a forest of white firs and sugar pines before reaching a clearing that gave me a view of Bald Mountain standing off in the distance to the northwest.

Above and to the right of the mountain was Grizzly Peak, a point I hoped to be reaching in a couple of days.

These hopes faded a bit, when later on I realized that I was off-course.

Somehow I'd wandered off in the wrong direction and my continual easterly course didn't tally-up with what should have been happening. I struggled commendably to make the terrain fit the map, but to no avail, and I eventually had to admit to myself that Wrong-Way Spearing had done it again.

My new course was taking me along the banks of a picturesque creek, and pleasant as it was, my next scheduled creek should have been at least eleven kilometres away.

To add to the urgency, I had started dogging the tracks of a rather large bear that had also followed the same course that I was now on. I rapidly retraced my steps until I was satisfied that I was near the point that I had gone wrong.

Sure enough after casting around I found the turning point I should have taken, obscured by dense undergrowth that concealed a bend in the trail.

I finally reached the headwaters of Moosehead Creek after adding an unnecessary 7kms to my day and began pitching my tent in the mottled light of the covering trees.

I had the feeling that I was not alone, and looking around spotted a lone mule deer, standing silently about fifteen metres away and watching me intently.

She was a curious creature, seeming to enjoy my company as much as I enjoyed hers, for she hung around for at least two hours, approaching to within five metres of me but coming no further. She didn't seem the least bit nervous though and casually wandered about in front of me, her head cocked, watching me with intelligent eyes as I babbled on at her with topics that I thought might be of interest to a deer of her calibre.

She wasn't very hungry, and ignored the offerings from my evening meal that I tossed to her. She even left my tasty anti-bear urine circle intact and disappeared just on dusk, when I bade her goodnight and crawled into my tent.

To someone like me who spends most of his time in a city, these moments of contact with wild creatures were pure magic and made for some good memories.

My only concern was that one day, the friendliness of this particular creature would make her an easy hit for someone with a taste for venison.

My trail started again as usual around dawn, and after a thirty nine kilometre hike that took me past Grizzly Peak, the point I'd sighted in the distance just under two days ago, I descended to spend the night on the banks of the McLoud River, meeting up with a couple of trout fishermen from San Francisco.

The pair were hospitable company and I suspect that their pick-up held more grog than fishing gear. The following morning I emerged from my tent slightly more bleary-eyed than usual, and clutching three cans of beer that they had pressed upon me, I stumbled off in the direction of Girard Ridge, 32kms away.

Despite the generous anaesthetics provided by the merry anglers the night before, I hadn't slept too well. My thermarest ground pad had sprung a leak, and I seemed to have spent most of the night re-adjusting myself on the hard ground, feeling every lump and bump like a full-length braille reader. Another fixit job for my, "must do" list.

After a crossing of Fitzhugh Gulch, Trough Creek and Squaw Valley Creek, a final hot ascent landed me on top of Girard Ridge. This was my last campsite before descending to the Sacramento River and the small settlement of Castella over 2500 feet (762m) and about seventeen kilometres away below me.

To the north, a magnificent view of Mount Shasta presented itself, and I mentally gave myself a solid boot up the khyber for using the last of my film at the McLoud River. I consoled myself with the thought that photos are never as good as the real thing and settled down to watch the changing colours as the sun disappeared from Girard Ridge.

Stephen Girard was a young French sea captain who had settled in Philadelphia during the Revolutionary Wars after the Brits had blockaded US ports.

He subsequently built up a strong trading fleet and couldn't have been too short of a dollar or two, because in 1812 he actually *bought out* the Bank of the United States, renaming it after himself.

Being French, as well as having been messed around by the British, it would probably be fair to say that he didn't have too much time for the Brits, and towards the end of the War of 1812 when US credit was at its lowest ebb, he subscribed to 95 per cent of the government war loan. This enabled the US to carry on the fight against the British with the ultimate desired affect.

With a CV like that, having a ridge named after you is no big deal...I would have expected a state at least!

I duly arrived at Castella at 1000 the next morning, and after spending an hour sitting on the ground outside Ammirati's supermarket consuming a family-size box of cereal, two pints of milk, a box of doughnuts, two apples and a snicker bar, I dragged myself away from Alladin's culinary cave to uplift my supply parcel from the post office. Having sorted and stowed my parcel, I decided to give my dirty clothes a treat and take them to a laundromat - their muffled screams for water could be heard emerging from my pack like some mafia victim incarcerated in the boot of a car.

As I stuffed the grateful articles into a machine, an attractive young lady next to me struck up a conversation, asking where I'd come from. I gave her the details.

"Gee, what a great life. I wish I was coming with you!"

I must admit that her off-hand remark had a certain appeal to it, but I resisted the sudden urge to invite her along. Which was just as well, for seconds later her boyfriend who was a twelve foot tall, two hundred pound version of a young Jack Palance, loomed through the door.

I returned my attention to the spinning clothes and thought of England.

That afternoon, Ziggy, The Gimp and Vern, (who had recovered from his bout of illness since our meeting in Belden) turned up. We were busy swapping the latest news when we were joined by Milt, one of the locals.

Milt Kenny was a great old guy, he must have been at least eighty. He was just a little fellow whose stature belied the fact that he had once been a lumberjack, and still had one of the most powerful handshakes I'd ever struck. He was quite an identity in these parts and even had a local trail named after him.

His kindness was well known amongst those who used the PC trail, and while doing my research back in NZ I had actually read an article about the trail that had mentioned him.

He never took anyone back to his place, but if you asked for any assistance, he'd always do his best to help you out. We'd asked where the best diner was and how to get to it.

Straight away we were all piled into his car and he escorted us into a local hamburger bar and insisted in buying us each a feed. As much as I appreciated his offer, I declined. He must have been on some kind of pension, and I just felt that I'd be taking advantage of his generosity. I hope I didn't offend him.

The Gimp had been having recurring problems with his boots. He couldn't seem to get a pair that didn't mangle his feet and had already abandoned one pair and was looking for a third.

I couldn't figure that one out. For someone who had obviously done as much hiking as he had, I would have thought that he'd have sorted out a compatible make of boot by now.

Apparently not. Milt offered to drive him into Dunsmuir, a more sizeable place about ten or eleven kilometres further north where he might have some luck. I tagged along for the ride, and kept Milt company while The Gimp searched around for some replacement footwear.

His search had been unsuccessful and he returned to the car in a black mood, which was the only time I'd seen him like that. He asked Milt to wait, and strode off to a nearby pay phone muttering about having to ring home and arrange for a, "freakin' pair of boots" to be dispatched.

I don't know who he was talking to on the phone, but his long and loud conversation was turning the air around the phone booth blue. Whoever they were, The Gimp was giving them both barrels at full volume. Just as well old Milt had been a lumberjack, Gimp's tirade was enough to make a marine blush.

Milt kept looking at his watch, "How long's he gonna be? I want to get home and have somethin' to eat!"

I was feeling a bit awkward about his agitation after his kindnesses to us, and was glad when the Gimp finally slammed down the phone and we could get going again.

Milt dropped us off and I farewelled the Gimp, taking off to camp for the night near the state park's ablution block. I was heading on next morning and wanted to spend some time patching up my leaking ground pad. It hadn't been dark for long when Milt turned up to say goodbye.

We talked for a while and he showed me an old photo of his late wife that he carried around in his wallet. I think he still missed her quite a bit.

Sadly, Milt has since passed away. Wherever he is now I hope he's happy.

Milt Kenny was one of the gentlemen of the trail.

My next lot of supplies were at Seiad Valley 251kms and six days away, and the first of those long days took me through the Castle Craggs Wilderness that seemed to have more than its fair share of climb. This was followed by a traverse of the invisible boundary line dividing Trinity and Siskiyou counties, passing two lakes that lay below me in the glacial cirque of the Mumbo Basin and eventually reaching familiar sounding Upper Gumboot Lake - I half expected to meet Fred Dagg and his Taihape mates when I got there.

Always the opportunist, I lay beside my tent studying my maps to see if I could spot a shortcut to make tomorrow a bit easier. After all those miles, I wasn't much of a purist when it came to sticking rigidly to the PC trail. Although the opportunities were few and far between, if another trail presented a better or more interesting alternative, then I'd grab it.

Sure enough, about eleven kilometres ahead, above Toad Lake, a trail branched away to the north in the general direction of Bear Creek, fording a couple of creeks and a river to drop me back on the PC at Bull Lake.

I rightly figured that it would cut a couple of hours off my day and get me the respectable distance to Masterton Meadows, and although the going turned out to be a bit confusing and rough at times, it was worth the effort. Not the least because at one stage I passed through a swampy area that was wall to wall with carnivorous Pitcher plants.

These plants were selling for a small fortune in NZ and here they were in their thousands growing like weeds! A random inspection showed that they were full of bugs and happily digesting and burping away.

Thankfully they hadn't tapped into the Big Pine Cone genes of further south. Ending up on a vegetables menu would have been a bit *too* weird.

Tracking southward through the Scott Mountains, I eventually entered the Trinity Alps Wilderness.

It was in this region that the controversial Patterson video was filmed near Bluff creek. Patterson and a cohort had shot some footage of a supposed Sasquatch after it had spooked their horses and then sauntered off looking back over its shoulder.

I've seen the video clip on television a few times over the years, and to me old Big Foot looked suspiciously like some joker wearing a fur coat and a balaclava.

I kept my camera handy - I've been known to be wrong!

Leaving the Shasta-Trinity Forest and entering the Klamath National Forest un-Sasquatched, I made my way across Forest Road 93 and camped in the trees that grew on a flat area above it.

It wasn't quite dark but I'd already eaten and was lying in my tent when something crashing through the undergrowth caused me to tense and stop breathing. "Oh no, not more bloody bears!"

This thought was immediately followed by a, "Hullo!" shouted from the direction of the noise.

Either I was being stalked by a particularly cunning and articulate sort of bear or I was about to be visited by a human or an educated Yeti.

I silently peered out of my tent and could see a figure casting around in the dimming light and slowly heading in my direction. He looked slightly on the desperado side, so I watched him for a while, contemplating whether or not to reveal my whereabouts.

He paused and called out again. If he maintained his course he was probably going to spot me at any moment anyhow, so I returned his call and he headed over.

Tony turned out to be a real nice character, with a slow and friendly drawl that reminded me of the character in the lead role of McLoud, an old TV cop show.

He was an ex-Vietnam chopper pilot, flying periodically for the forestry service.

182

That day he'd been engaged in an aerial search for a couple of lost hikers who had eventually been found. He'd spotted my tent through the trees and had become curious.

"Thought you might like one of these!", he produced a couple of beers and handed me one.

"You got a double y'know that?! When you stuck your head outta that tent I thought you was a buddy of mine. You guys could be brothers!"

This confirmed that not only was Tony a friendly character, but that he also hung out with some pretty smooth looking dudes!

He and his father ran a small sawmill and they were in the middle of a drama that was threatening their livelihoods. Some outfit had milled some of their trees by mistake and were now threatening them with, "the death of their mill" if they made a claim against them. They were going to fight though.

"How many hours does it take to get your chopper licence?", I asked. He gave a slow grin, "Depends if there's a war on, better have plenty of time and $35,000 in your pocket if there ain't!"

Apparently he'd had no previous experience of flying before being drafted into the army during the Vietnam conflict. It had been a tough training ground and an unpopular war, but some good had come of it, in that he had ended up with a skill that carried into civilian life.

We talked for about an hour before he wished me well and disappeared off through the trees again. I added another American to the list of potential visitors to NZ that might turn up on my doorstep one day.

The trail swung northwest with views back down into deep South Fork Lakes Canyon before heading north again 1200ft above deep Jackson Lake that lay to the east.

Crossing a saddle I entered into the Russian Wilderness, treading a trail that had been blasted across the cliffs. A massive granite wall helped give the impression of being back in the High Sierras again and I could

183

feel some of the old magic returning as I pushed on, finally leaving the Russian Wilderness area and making camp just past Etna Summit in the Marble Mountain Wilderness.

Flat ground seemed to be scarce around here, and digging out a level platform for the tent I wished I wasn't so damn fussy about my sleeping habits.

Talking of digging, the majority of the trail sections particularly in the more popular areas were well maintained, and I was pleased to meet up with some of the people that did the job. A forestry trail gang were working on the slopes above Shotgun Gulch, sweating in the heat as they dug out and re-aligned a section of the trail.

Their camp was further along the trail near Shelly Meadows and Tom, one of the young workers, told me that although he enjoyed the work he was looking forward to heading out in a couple of weeks to see his girl.

I knew the problem, and asked him what his girl friend thought of his absences.

"Don't bother her too much, she's got some fights on at the moment." That was a comment that intrigued me and needed further investigation. It turned out that she was a boxer in training for a lead up to a title fight.

"Doesn't it bother you that she might be getting her face re-arranged?"

"Naw, she can handle herself okay."

She sounded like a formidable lady who certainly blew the myth of the domesticated little woman waiting at home doing the knitting and baking apple pies!

I had visions of her tending to one of their future sobbing off-spring after accidentally bopping it, "Of course mommy loves you! Just remember to keep your guard up when someone rings the doorbell honey."

After a sleepless night being nuisanced by deer at Marble Valley, I lost altitude to camp at Grider Creek, just 10kms out of the small settlement of Seiad Valley.

A mile or so before reaching the creek I fell into step with Rich who was returning to the trail-head after giving his injured leg a test run.

Rich was a sawmill worker from Idaho now working in Seiad. He'd been laid up for some time with a leg injury and had wanted to make sure that it could take the pressure before starting back to work. He seemed happy with the result.

I commented that Idaho was a fair way from Seiad Valley.

"Well, you go where the work is," he replied.

I knew that the milling industry was having some problems with conservationists trying to drastically reduce logging operations, and I asked him about this.

He looked unhappy, "Well, loggers gotta eat, but jobs could be going as conservationists are trying to stop the trees comin' down on account of the Little Spotted Owl that they're tryin' to save. Boy, they sure get fired up over that damn bird!"

This gem of information was slotted away in the back of my head, and further north in Oregon I was able to pull it out to create a little bit of mischief.

We parted at the trail-head, and he drove off after kindly providing me with some cheese, water and two cans of soft drink.

I crossed over the Klamath River not long after dawn and arrived at the Seiad diner in time for breakfast.

The place was wall to wall hikers!

Ziggy, The Gimp, Vern, plus two other familiar faces, Brian and his off-sider Dave.

I'd spent an entertaining night camped with the latter duo further south. They were a memorable pair. Dave was a dead ringer for a young Burt Lancaster, and Brian who'd not long come out of the 101st

Airborne Regiment was built like the proverbial brick out-house. Their idea of a leisurely hike was to march along doing bicep curls with some large rock that they'd picked up, interspersed with sudden stops for a session of press-ups when the rock lifting got boring.

"You gotta work out your upper body George, this hiking only does your legs!"

I'd paused to look at the two thread-like limbs that were hanging from my shoulders and decided that they could stay that way until I reached Canada. I needed every calorie of energy just to keep my legs swinging backwards and forwards, and with the amount of weight I was losing, even these were threatening to snap off and stick up my bum.

Their exuberance reminded me of the old adage of the young bull and the old bull. On the remote chance you've never heard it, it goes something like this...

Two bulls were strolling along a ridge and looked down to spot a load of cows in the paddock below.

"All right!", says the young bull, "What say we run down and make love to a couple of 'em!"

"Naw," says the old bull, "Let's *walk* down and make love to *all* of 'em!"

Like the old bull, I intended conserving energy for the long haul!

Brian was a big fan of New Zealand and Australia.

Rightly or wrongly (depending on what you know) he was impressed with the, "green" image that a lot of the world has of NZ.

"An' I'll tell you what," he said, "all the world's at one and others throat, wheelin' dealin' and trying to kill each other. And then there's you good guys down in the southern hemisphere, just gettin' on with life and leavin' everyone alone!"

He wasn't quite so impressed with the Brits. He'd spent some time in the U.K. on a joint US/British military exercise and had run into some trouble.

"Man there's somethin' wrong with those Limeys. They got a big chip or somethin' on their shoulders about how we bailed them out in the Second World War. Every time we met up in a bar they'd wanna start fightin'!"

I could just imagine the volatile combination. Alcohol, young soldiers, a comment passed on, "how you limeys needed us to get you out of the poo", and whammo, national and regimental pride would be at stake! She'd be all on for the duration of the exercise - what else could happen! I was relieved that he saw me as a good guy Kiwi, and tactfully refrained from telling him that I was actually born a Brit.

Seiad Valley was the last settlement in California, and making the most of it, we spent a leisurely day kicking back, swapping lies and bouncing around the usual banter, before heading out en masse at 1640.

The dynamic duo were doing their usual trailside callisthenics, but this time they were copping a bit of good-humoured flack from the troops. Finishing a quick ten press-ups they carried on their way, Dave looking hurt and muttering, "...we could do without the freakin' peanut gallery".

It was a long 15 mile haul up to the Cook and Green Saddle where we all camped for the night, climbing at times to almost 6000ft above Seiad Valley. By the time we stopped it was 2100hrs and long past my normal bedtime!

I was just about to hit the pit when Vern came over for a bit of a natter, "I've decided on a good nickname for you George."

My curiosity was aroused, "What is it?"

"Cougar."

Wow! That was pretty cool! Why did he call me that I wondered.

Was it because of the cougar-like way that I stealthily and silently ranged the mountains, my lithe and muscular body flitting sure-footedly amongst the trees?!

"Why do you reckon I should be called cougar Vern?"

"Because the pattern on your boot soles leave a print like a cougar."

I felt a bit deflated. "Oh well," I thought, hiding my disappointment as I retired for the night, at least he hadn't picked up on my navigational prowess and called me Wrong Way Spearing...

The lovely Carola, surrounded by dangerous levels of testosterone.

After three months – the California/Oregon border

Another snowy Pass

From hot Mojave desert...

To cold Sierra Nevada snow

Ziggy modeling his racing knees, and The Gimp

Sheer luxury at the Mojave's edge

Cascades

A Rae Lakes Marmot awaits his lunch

Cascade Range, Washington

Lake, Indian Heaven Wilderness, Washington

Old cabin, Plumas Forest, California

Into the Sierra Nevada

Chapter Eight
Oregon

Ashland, Hillary, Crater Lake, Lolo latrine, Columbia River.

The next day our differing paces and needs had spread us out, and on July 31st I eventually left California at Donomore Meadows east of Donomore Peak and crossed into Oregon.

A small weathered wooden sign marked, "California/Oregon" had been nailed to a tree by someone to mark the spot.

This was a real milestone. After 102 days on the trail and having walked over 2832 kilometres, I now considered myself to be well and truly over half-way towards my goal.

Musing over the experiences of the past three months, I realized that I hadn't yet ever considered packing it in, but there had been times, particularly around the 1000km mark where I'd questioned the sanity of all this hard yakka and wondered if my lift wasn't quite making it to the top floor.

But the entire state of California was behind me now, I was on a roll and totally invincible!

The next minute I was flat on my back with my legs sticking up unfrontiersman-like in the air.

I'd been walking backwards getting a last look at California and had managed to trip over Oregon.

Oh well, even cougars can get it wrong sometimes.

After a night camped at Sheep Springs and a day travelling through the Siskiyou Mountains I dropped down to Interstate 5.

I was leaving the trail here for a while, to detour into the delights of Ashland town.

Besides being a reward for getting through California in one piece, it was also the supply point for my next food parcel and hopefully a new pair of boots. My present boots had served me well but the tread on the soles was disappearing at an alarming rate of knots, and the subsequent lack of grip had been the cause of several Torvil and Dean impressions that I'd been entertaining the fauna with lately.

Sometime further back I'd mailed a request to fellow firefighter and friend John Tuke, asking if he could mail me out a pair of replacement Asolo boots. I'd thought about having my old ones re-soled, but the uppers were beginning to split across the top from the continual flexing and I still had a good 1609 kms to go. If I kept them, I'd probably end up crossing the Canadian border with my boots flapping like a pair of castanets.

I looked at my map, and with a sinking heart realized that it must have been at least another 10 miles from here into Ashland.
Ten minutes by automobile. Over three hours by footmobile - Bugger!
I'd taken only a few steps in the direction of Ashland when a car pulled up alongside me.
"Going into town? Get in!"
My saviour was Hillary Varaday, a lady in a big straw hat and hippy-style dress. She lived in an apartment block with her teenage son Warwick, young daughter Merlin, and a ballet dancer that was out of town for a while.
"Where are you going to stay?"
I told her that I'd probably find somewhere to put up a tent for the night and was delighted when she offered me the use of the couch at her place for the duration of my stay.
This was landing on your feet!

Her apartment was next to a twenty-four hour supermarket, minutes from the town centre, and the next-door neighbours were all dead.
"Doesn't it bother you living alongside a cemetery", I asked.

"No, I've spoken to the spirits there and they're all at peace."

She wasn't kidding, Hillary was different. She gave me a taped copy of her poems that she'd produced for sale. She had a melodic and soothing voice, and even now the tape can rocket me back to Ashland in the blink of an eye.

I showered and changed into my, "clean" cotton shirt and track pants.

"Your feet must be sore after all those miles, would you like me to give you a foot massage?"

It occurred to me that I must have died on the trail and somehow been mis-routed into heaven. I lay back in contentment, a happy hiker, wondering how difficult it was to get permanent residency.

Ashland is a pleasant town of about 17,000 people, lying at the southern end of the Rogue River Valley in Jackson county.

It had developed as a lumber town but also relied heavily on encouraging tourism - I think Hillary should have been awarded the tourism boards' Medal of Honour for her PR work above and beyond the call of duty!

I was sitting outside the post office lacing up the new boots that John had mailed out to me, when I was joined by Ziggy and the Gimp. The Gimp was moving off again that day, but the cerebral Ziggy was hanging around to attend the local Shakespearean festival.

This bit of information supplied us with screeds of laughter, as we invented scenarios where the skinny knobbly-kneed Ziggy clad in sagging Shakespearean tights forsook a randy Juliet in favour of a pizza-to-go and a goblet of hash-browns.

"Lady, by yonder blessed moon I swear,
Just one more pizza an' I'm outta there!"
Beauty is bought by judgement of the eye,
Just twang your lute while I scoff this pie."

After a donation from the Gimp of some elixir that he'd been waterproofing his tent with, Ziggy and I wished him farewell then went our separate ways to enjoy our chosen trappings of civilization for yet another day.

I was asked by Hillary if I'd like to take part in an Indian sweat house ceremony, or would I prefer to go to the movies.

To my eternal regret I chose the movies.

At the time, the idea of sitting in a sauna when I was desperately trying to build up some fat reserves, didn't ring my bell.

So instead of losing weight in an Indian sweat house, which was probably the only chance I'll ever get to be able to say that I'd experienced "cultural *enlightenment*" in its most literal form, I ended up watching Patrick Swayze poncing about as a lovesick ghost, and throwing popcorn and ice cream down my neck.

I left Ashland the following morning, and after giving Hillary, Warwick and Merlin a small gift each, I loaded my pack into her old car and Hillary drove me back to the point she'd picked me up from.

Just before leaving, she handed me a small stone that she'd picked up from outside her apartment, "Would you do me a favour?"

"Of course."

"When you return to your country, would you bury this stone there somewhere?"

"No problem."

I watched as she drove off down the road and silently thanked her again for her kindness and for making Ashland a place to remember. A little piece of Ashland now lives buried on One Tree Hill in Auckland.

My next port of call was the post office at Crater Lake National Park headquarters, 177 kms and five days away. At the time, Crater Lake was not strictly on the Pacific Crest trail, but I'd heard that it was such an awesome sight that the detour would be worth it. (An alternate

198

route has since been made, ascending Dutton Creek trail to take you along the rim.)

I slowly shook loose the lethargy of civilization and got back into wilderness mode as the trail annoyingly wound its way south, heading back towards Mexico before eventually getting its act together and swinging northwards once again.

Despite their reputation for having a higher rainfall, I looked forward to hiking Oregon and Washington.

I figured that I would be able to clock up higher mileages on account of their lower elevations.

The average trail altitude through California had been 6000ft, whilst in these next two states it was only 5000ft and 4000ft respectively.

My highest point in California had been a snow filled world of around 13,000ft. In Oregon I would only climb to just over 7,500ft, and although it can snow at any time of the year along the Oregon and Washington trail, I didn't expect to see much of it if I made the Canadian border before October.

This section of the trail between here and Crater Lake was pretty dry as far as creeks and lakes went. A quick squiz at my map showed that the Sky Lakes Wilderness area was absolutely chocker with lakes of varying sizes just lying around waiting to be slurped, but the PC trail obstinately threaded its way through the lot of them, keeping as far away as possible!

I made a couple of minor adjustments to my route and took the Rye Spur, Badger Lake and Sky Lakes trails to ensure a decent water supply, then re-joined the PCT at Devils Peak where an abandoned section of the old Oregon Skyline trail linked up with it.

Six kilometres on I filled my water bottles at Honeymoon Creek, the last easily available water for about 40 kms and headed on past Maude Mountain and Lone Wolf Mountain to cross the Oregon desert and eventually enter the Crater Lakes National Park.

Oregon, "desert" is a bit of a misnomer really, as it's actually forested with lodgepole pines. But as far as water was concerned it was a desert.

All the creeks in the area had been covered in a layer of pumice and ash about seven thousand years ago when neighbouring Mount Mazama blew itself to pieces forming Crater Lake and making life thirstier for me.

The trail hit Highway 62 and I detoured towards Annie Springs, the Goodbye Picnic area and Crater Lake.

Passing the picnic area I approached a parked car, shimmering in the mid-day heat and sporting a Californian number plate and two open doors.

From the noise coming out of it, it was obvious that the two occupants in the front seats were having a bad day.

The male driver was in danger of imitating Mount Mazama as he thumped the steering wheel to emphasise his words, "WELL MAKE UP YOUR GODDAM MIND!! DO WE GET TO SEE THE LAKE OR NOT!! "

I pulled alongside just as the woman in the passenger seat let fly with a paper cupful of drink that she had been holding, bouncing it off the drivers head and giving him a preview of what the lake was like.

Fascinated, I slowed my pace and watched as he slicked back his wet hair, slammed his door shut, hurled the cup out the window and fired up the engine.

"THAT'S IT!! WE'RE GOIN' HOME!!"

The car did a rapid U turn and disappeared off down the road.

The last I saw of the happy campers as they sped towards their Californian love-nest, was the arm of the woman stretching out and trying to close her swinging door.

I continued on my carefree way...my life wasn't so tough after all.

In June of 1853 prospector John Wesley Hillman almost took a one thousand foot freestyle dive into Crater Lake when his mule suddenly slammed on all four brakes and came to a screaming stop.

He'd become the first recorded white man to discover the six mile wide 1932ft deep, intensely blue lake, and after a bit of careful thought he named it Deep Blue Lake. Sixteen years later he was probably a bit put out when his inventively named lake was re-christened with the name it has today.

As I'd been rightly told, it was an awesome sight.

It must have been one hell of a bang when the top blew off to create a pond of this size and I wasn't surprised to learn that the ash fall-out landed as far afield as Saskatchewan in Canada.

There are no outlets running from it and any fish that inhabit the lake have been introduced.

Wizard Island, a small outcrop in the middle, popped up after a later much smaller eruption.

Typically, this lake was another of the sights that I'd experienced that couldn't be done justice with my small camera - the panoramic grandeur of things could take your breath away, but a sector of them reproduced through the narrow vision of my camera lens reduced them to nothing. I contented myself with an aerial postcard.

The area around the Rim Village was alive with tourists and vehicles, and as usual when I'd suddenly burst upon, "civilization" after a stint in the woods, I was just a little overwhelmed.

Feeling a bit like the odd-man-out amongst all the well dressed and well groomed visitors swooping here and there with their cameras,

I was just about to shoulder my pack and head off again when a middle-aged couple approached me.

"Didn't we see you walking up that steep road to get here?"

"Yeah, I suppose that would've been me."

(A couple of vehicles had kindly stopped to offer me a lift on the steep climb, but I'd refused knowing that I wouldn't be returning to the trail the same way, and my mission after all, was to walk all the way to Canada.)

The woman looked at me, "You mean you walked *all* the way up that road with that heavy pack?"

"Well actually, I've walked all the way up from Mexico."

She looked at me as if I was from another planet. Her husband stared at me and slowly shook his head,

"You kind of guys usually have a story to tell, what's yours, why are you doing it?"

That one threw me. The expectant way he was looking at me, I felt like he was waiting for me to either disclose a dramatic story of unrequited love, a profound discourse on the search for the meaning of life, or that my name was Richard Kimble and I was on the run and looking for a man with one arm or something!

I felt like I was letting down a whole regiment of, "You kind of guys" when the best I could come up with was a bland and totally boring, "I just wanted to see if I could do it."

The lady lifted up her video camera, "D'you mind if I get a shot?"

I was totally bemused, "No, if that's what you want!"

By now a small group had gathered around to hear what this unshaven character was on about and I was fielding the usual questions. A small boy amongst them pulled at his mother's sleeve as she looked on,

"Mom is that man a cowboy?"

Considering that I was wearing shorts, the idea appealed to my sense of humour, and I envisaged myself walking into a wild west saloon to be greeted by the barman....

"Howdy stranger. Hear tell yore the only cowpoke in these parts wearin' short pants."

"Yep. Reckon that's why folks hereabouts call me Georgie The Kid."

I laughed, and the woman looked embarrassed and hustled away with the kid in tow.

I was beginning to feel a bit awkward with all the attention I was suddenly getting, and with a "Well gotta get going", I hefted my pack and moved off.

As I passed an elderly man that had been quietly standing to one side away from the group, he nodded unsmilingly at me and said, "I admire your guts son and envy what you're doing."

....My feet didn't touch the ground for the rest of the day, and I floated off into the woods with a pack that felt as light as a feather to camp next to Dutton Creek.

Re-supply could have been a problem along this next stretch of the trail, but I was headed for a Seventh Day Adventist youth camp just over 257 kms away at the northern end of the Mt.Washington Wilderness, where I'd hopefully find my supplies awaiting pick-up.

The main problem around here seemed to be those damn mosquitoes again, but I was suitably armed with repellant now, and apart from the continual buzzing in the ears as they made abortive dives on me, I wasn't too hassled by them.

What I was *always* on the lookout for, especially at the lower altitudes that horses, deer or cattle frequented, were ticks.

These obnoxious little sods would inhabit the vegetation lying in wait for you and then leaping on to you as you brushed past.

They'd then crawl around selecting a spot to their liking before painlessly burrowing in and gorging themselves on your blood.

You had to be extremely careful extracting them and try not to leave their heads behind or you would increase the chances of infection.

The two worst infections that you could get from these ticks were the gloriously named Rocky Mountain Spotted Fever, and the appetising sounding Lymes Disease.

Rocky Mountain Spotted Fever I was cheerfully informed, had symptoms resembling typhoid.

If I experienced insomnia, disorientation and delirium, then I wasn't to worry too much about it, because for the next stage I'd probably be slipping into a coma and wouldn't feel anything before I croaked a week later.

Lymes Disease on the other hand was quite benevolent really, letting you live on for many years with nothing more than memory and vision disturbances, crippling arthritis and symptoms resembling Multiple Sclerosis.

Ticks made a full-on attack by a psychotic bear seem quite welcome in comparison.

Because of their painless incursions into your skin, you didn't always know that you'd picked one up until it was well and truly ensconced. Added to the problem was the fact that they seemed to prefer warm, moist, out-of-the-way locations to start their burrowing.

I'd already extracted two of these repulsive mites from myself. One from the back of my leg underneath my sock, and the other as it happily burrowed into my crotch.

It's not a happy moment sitting in the middle of nowhere with your shorts around your ankles, frantically blowing and elbowing mosquitoes out of the way whilst ants bite your bum and you try to get a pair of tweezers around a creature that's intent on disappearing up your soft bits.

It builds more character than I had ever imagined possible.

Mt.Thielson Wilderness was not surprisingly the home of Mt.Thielson, where a couple of days after leaving Crater Lake I climbed to around 7,300ft to skirt its western slopes before descending to Thielson Creek to refill my water bottles.

A lone tent was pitched alongside the creek, and not particularly feeling like socialising, I toyed with the idea of giving it a miss. However, the heat of the day and the sight of rushing crystal water proved too much of a magnet and I descended to be greeted by Mike and his girlfriend, the two occupants of the camp.

Mike was a firefighter from Roseburg, a small town in southwestern Oregon.

They'd planned to take a week's break in the mountains, but it looked as though their stay was going to be shortened by a couple of days - it doesn't seem to be a good idea to have things dangling off the outside of a pack if you can help it, and they'd discovered this to their misfortune after they'd managed to lose some of their supplies off the back of theirs.

I filled my bottles, and with a promise to keep an eye out for their lost supplies and to leave them in a prominent position if I found them, set off in the direction of Odell Lake in the Diamond Peak Wilderness. Studying my maps at Windigo Pass, I decided to leave the northwesterly winding PCT and head northeasterly along the old Oregon Skyline Trail.

Besides appearing to be a more direct route towards my target of Odell Lake, it also loosely followed the course of Whitefish Creek, Trapper Creek and a few assorted lakes.

This meant that the eternal problem of water supply was soundly dealt to.

I reached Cascade Summit, a trail head on the edge of Odell Lake the following morning.

The going had been pleasant enough over wooded if at times swampy ground, and as usual at trail heads there were more signs of people - one manifestation being a camp fire that had been left merrily smouldering away by some dork or dorkette unknown.

I crossed Highway 58 at Willamette Pass and after four days of scenic travel through the woods and lava beds of the Three Sisters and Mount Washington Wilderness areas, made camp in a flat forested area north of McKenzie Pass and just four hours walk away from my supply parcel at the Seventh Day Adventist camp at Big Lake in Hidden

Valley.

The volcanic lava beds surrounding the slopes of Belknap crater and McKenzie Pass had provided a totally different outing for my senses. After months of experiencing nothing but green vegetation or white snow, the total blackness of the terrain, devoid of plants, was like walking across the surface of some alien planet.

Just quietly, I was happy to get back into the good old trees again.

The area may well have been extinct, but it gave me the feeling that the ground was just waiting for a suitable candidate before opening up and introducing him to Dante's inferno.

Not having led a *totally* exemplary life, I had an uneasy feeling that I might just have qualified for a bit of unwanted heat treatment.

As it was, the area already held the remains of at least one unlucky pioneer.

In 1873 John Templeton Craig finished labouring on a road to link eastern and western Oregon. He'd done a lot of the work alone, and was probably quite chuffed when four years later he was given the job of carrying the mails over his road.

He must have had time to reflect on the irony of grafting all those years on a road that was to lead to his end, when he was trapped by a blizzard in a cabin near McKenzie Pass. His body was found weeks later.

Bit of a bummer to have survived years of road building in the wilderness only to get a postman's job and then get wiped out on your first delivery round.

John Craig left his bones behind - I left Janet's black camera case behind.

I spent about an hour retracing my steps and searching for it, but it was a bit like looking for a yellow button in a field of buttercups and I eventually gave up.

Thankfully, my carelessness didn't incur the wrath of Janet on my return to NZ, and she accepted the loss with a surprisingly philosophical shrug of the shoulders.

Passing the western side of Mount Washington, with its barren summit block sticking up like a ravaged jagged molar, I eventually began a salivating descent through the trees in the direction of Big Lake's youth camp and food.

I paused, just ahead of me I spotted the bulky figure of a crossbow hunter making his way stealthily along the trail and scanning the surrounding terrain.

I watched him silently for a while just in case he was actually on to something. Seeing that he was not, and not wanting to end up like a porcupine, I made my presence known and approached him.

He stood a muscular six foot plus, was decked out in full camouflage gear and carried a cocked and lethal looking crossbow.

He also had the guiltiest look on his face of anyone I'd seen, barring perhaps the star in a Nuremburg Trial documentary, or a cat with the pet goldfish in its mouth.

"How's it goin'? Had any luck?"

He looked decidedly guarded, "Naw, I'm not huntin' for anythin', just doing a bit of target shooting to keep my eye in."

(Yeah good one mate, must be pretty jittery targets around here if you have to sneak up on them dressed like a tree!)

He was obviously a bit wary of my credentials, so I made it known that my only interest was in making headway north and he relaxed a bit.

Sure enough, he was out hunting, but he was out of season for a crossbow or didn't have a permit or something, so he'd been a bit careful until he'd known who he was talking to.

I left him to it, once more glad that I wasn't hairier and wearing my antler hat.

I duly arrived at the youth camp and picked up my parcel that had been kindly held free of charge for me. My two hour stay at the camp was quite a refreshing experience really.

The positive and cheerful kindness of the youthful interns and their leaders was quite uplifting, and nothing seemed to be too much trouble for them.

I was given a cheap though excellent meal in their dining hall, and a free re-fill of white spirits for my camp stove.

I have a sneaking suspicion though, that some of them may have thought that they were doing their bit to ease the burden of an old tramp.

One of the young ladies who was watching me devour my meal as though it may have been taken away from me at any moment, smiled sweetly and out of the blue asked, "How do you manage to live with no money?"

I had to explain that I had plenty of money and even a job, but that I always looked like that when I was on leave. It was one of the perks of not being married.

She didn't look too convinced, and was probably having some trouble getting her head around the fact that some people can voluntarily get themselves *that* hungry and *that* dilapidated!

I wandered off into steady rain with a full belly, a happy heart and another address added to my, "thank you" list.

My next supply parcel was waiting 250 kms away at the Columbia River, but I was hoping to supplement my food with a pick-up of something or other at the Timberline Lodge, which was only 169 kms away at the foot of Mount Hood.

My immediate concern was the rain. Unfortunately, it stuck with me more or less for the seven days it took me to reach the Columbia River. And for the next four days it rained continuously.

The rain was a low point, though it could have been a lot worse and I forced myself to look on it optimistically, reminding myself that it was infinitely better than being poked in the eye with a burnt stick.

Optimism aside, when you're outside in the rain for all that time, then *everything* gets soaked no matter how good your wet weather gear is. I'd do my best to try and keep my sleeping bag dry, but even that seemed to absorb the dampness out of the air.

Another downer, probably more psychological than anything else, was that damp gear and a wet tent added an extra pound or two to the weight you had to carry on your back.

Cooking, which had to be done outside in the open because my tent was too small and also because bears had such a ridiculously developed sense of smell, had become a write off.

Luckily, I'd anticipated rain in this region, and was carrying a lot of food that could be eaten uncooked. (Cheese, bread, salami, chocolate, raisins.)

I lay cold and dejected in my tent, eating a damp lump of bread and contemplating the small puddle that was slowly forming at my elbow as the wet ground gradually transferred itself through the floor in an attempt to test the absorption qualities of my sleeping bag.

This misery called for inspirational thinking, and as all the western movies I'd ever seen seemed to be unhelpfully filmed in locations where the hero never got rained on, my brain turned desperately to all the martial art movies I'd seen.

There was always some wrinkled little oriental guy of about ninety-five that gave profound esoterical advice to the young hero..."Remember Glasshopper, pain is in mind. Remove mind from body and pain will go."

At some stage in the movie, either the little wrinkled guy or the young hero would usually flatten a truck-load of Kalashnikov bearing bad guys with his bare hands, so I figured he might just be on to something.

I held my breath and squeezed my brain into a diner full of pancakes, maple syrup, fried eggs, hash browns, and gallons of hot coffee.

To hell with pain control, I was seeking a black belt in cholesterol.

My foray into esoteric mind control was a complete failure.

All it did was to give me a ravenous appetite and distract me enough to roll into the large icy puddle that had silently formed while I was trying to taste the mindburgers!

I've got my doubts about those little wrinkled oriental dudes.

My seven rainy days weren't all misery though and I managed to cheer myself up by briefly winding up a group of environmentalists that I'd chanced upon.

The worthy group had been plodding slowly along when I overtook them at Jude Lake.

They'd made their environmental interests obvious when they'd asked me if I'd seen any evidence of logging in the areas I'd passed through, and enthusiastically asked me what sort of birdlife I'd come across.

There was actually a fair bit of logging going on in Oregon, a shame really, as the big logging companies in for the dollar were stripping large areas of forest. These operations have caused some heated confrontations with environmentalists in the area.

It's a tricky situation. While it's not good to see the trees disappear, I can see the point of local loggers. It's their jobs that are on the line and the means of getting the food that fills the bellies of their families.

Some of those guys belong to generations of loggers or millers, and I guess it must get right up their noses to be told by some dude in from the city for a week, that they should stop doing what they do.

Anyhow, all the usual questions were asked of me, including, "What do you do for food when you're way out here?"

My mind flashed back to my meeting with Rich the sawmill worker just south of Seiad Valley and the information he'd given me on the conservationist campaign to save the Little Spotted Owl.

"No problem", I innocently replied, "When my food runs low, I just live mainly on berries and a little spotted owl thing that's dead easy to catch.

I just stone one, biff it in the pot and boil it up with a few berries and wild onions - quite tasty really, I call the dish Little *Potted* Owl."

The reaction was all I'd dreamed of, heads snapped around, brows furrowed and mouths dropped open before they realized that they were being sent up. I'd quickly decided that if I was to save myself from being lynched, I'd better laugh and show that I was only joking.

My spirits had also been further raised when I'd stopped briefly in the pouring rain to talk to a couple of Canadian hikers at Jeff Creek in the Mount Jefferson Wilderness.

These were the first two *Canadians* that I'd met since leaving Mexico and proof enough for me that I was finally approaching my northernmost destination!

Forty kilometres later, after a damp night camped at Clackamas Lake, I reached Timberline Lodge.

The lower glaciated slopes of Mount Hood adjoining the lodge were inspiring, even in the rain. Unfortunately the upper peak at 11,235ft was obscured by cloud and obstinately refused to reveal itself.

What care I though! The lodge, sitting at 6000ft was there for all to see, and what a magnificent building it was!

What's more, I thought, a structure of this size must undoubtedly be full of food!

I was expecting a large building, but this one was massive.

Built during the Great Depression of the thirties, one of its more recent claims to fame was that it had a starring role along with Jack Nicholson (who was also built during the Great Depression) in a scare movie called The Shining.

If I came across any little kids muttering, "redrum" then I was out of there. If you saw the movie you know what I mean!

I didn't even *try* to find out what the cost of a room was, but pitched my tent in a small patch of bush within sight and easy walking of the grand edifice and then sallied forth to check out the menus and look for some kind of food store to boost my almost non-existent supplies. I was disappointed.

There was no food store, all that was available was a variety of souvenirs, and not many of them were really edible. There was a store at Government Camp about 29 kms away, but this meant a two day hike to get there and back, or alternatively I could try and hitch a ride. Feeling slightly knackered and also knowing what my dubious success rate at getting lifts was, I didn't fancy either option.

Slightly daunted, my next move was to check out the restaurant prices, and after having done so, my Scottish blood had no hesitation in kicking the idea of a large steak dinner fairly out the door. I was hungry but not *that* hungry!

This left the hotel's fast food cafeteria. I used the hotels' auto teller to draw out some money on my Visa card and grudgingly forked out top dollar for some mediocre lukewarm food and one cup of tepid coffee. No refills here!

Maybe I'd just caught them on a bad day.

After confessing my ignorance on climbs around Mount Hood to a couple of tourists who assumed I looked like I should know about such things. I left the cafeteria and returned to my tent to sleep soundly, knowing that I was now only two days or so away from my supply parcel at Cascade Locks on the Columbia River.

The following morning I packed up my tent, bought some cheese, bread and a couple of turkey sandwiches from the Hotels' kitchen and headed off once more into the rain.

After crossing several creeks and canyons and pausing to appreciate attractive Ramona Falls, (which was difficult, as by now I was as wet as the falls and not in a particularly appreciative mood) I carried on to camp for the night at Lolo Pass.

Lolo Pass won the Most Distasteful Place Of The Journey award.

Besides being viewless because of cloud and saturated because of constant rain, it was also an open sewer because of the cretin shit that seemed to be everywhere you wanted to pitch a tent.

Lolo Pass was a trail, "head" in the nautical sense, as well as in the hiking sense. And as it had a secondary road running through it and was in fairly close proximity to the attraction of Timberline Lodge, it had been crapped upon by more than its fair share of moron campers. It was probably Giardia Headquarters for the entire state of Oregon. To complement the setting, high voltage power lines buzzed and crackled in the vicinity like Dr. Doom's Death Rays.

Camping at Lolo Pass is not for cissies - if you don't get typhoid or giardia from the cretin spoor, hang around long enough and you'll probably end up glowing from the bazillion megawatt electromagnetic field that radiates from the power lines!

It's been said that great adversity inspires great poetry.

As I lay in my tent blotting up the dampness, contemplating the meaning of life and eating a soggy turkey sandwich, I was inspired to compose this magnificent and movingly profound poetical gem;

Out west where you'll find Lolo Pass
You'll also find habits most crass,
Every step of your shoe will squish on a poo
That was shat by the crapulous mass.

I left at first light the next morning and after rounding the north spur of Indian Mountain in the Columbia Wilderness, left the PCT once more to take the steeply descending Indian Springs trail, which in turn led to the Eagle Creek trail.

The rain had finally stopped falling on my parade and as an added bonus, the drop in altitude had also brought a noticeable rise in temperature.

I'd heard that the Eagle Creek trail and its falls were worth the detour. I wasn't disappointed.

213

Eagle Creek was magic and lay at the bottom of a majestic and often vertical-sided gorge.

The trail that paralleled hundreds of feet above it was carved out of the steep canyon wall and was an awe-inspiring credit to those that had built it.

Tunnel Falls, a vertical sheet of water plummeting over the trail from high above, roared continuously as it plunged to the creek below. The trail made its way along a narrow ledge carved out of the canyon wall, to disappear *through* the rocky cliff face that was immediately behind the fall of water.

Like a lot of the experiences I'd encountered on this journey, Tunnel Falls was one of those that joined the list of things I'd found impossible to capture properly on film. This was because they were either too big, too close or just too intangible.

However, my imagination compensated for any lack of camera skills and as I approached the roaring falls along the narrow rock ledge I was suddenly transformed into a musical Indiana Jones, humming a loud and vigorous version of the theme tune from Raiders of the Lost Ark - in retrospect, it's probably a kind thing that there are not a lot of people around sometimes!

Emerging raider-like from behind the 150 foot drop of water, I carried on to pass some more attractive if not as spectacular falls and descended through cedar and Douglas fir forest to spend the night illegally camped at the Lower Punchbowl trail, only eight kilometres from the small town of Cascade Locks.

Cascade Locks lies on the southern bank of the wide Columbia River.

As a "cool" teenager, I'd bought a record by skiffle artist Lonnie Donnegan who'd sung about this river, and as I stood at last upon its banks it gave me a strange feeling that was almost like deja vu. My spirits were high, and I tracked the eight kilometres through the trees to

Cascade Locks slaughtering the only lines from the song that I could remember,

"The world holds seven wonders that the travellers often tell, some gardens and some towers, I guess you know them well.
But now the greatest wonder is in Uncle Sam's fair land, it's the mighty Columbia River
and the big Grand Coulee dam!"

The river I was serenading was christened by a trader, Robert Gray, who named it after his ship when he sailed up it in 1792, just a little before Lonnie cut his record.

The Columbia is an impressive stretch of water that begins life in the Canadian Rockies before flowing through Canada for 800km, then passing through the states of Washington and Oregon to complete its 2000km length by dumping into the Pacific Ocean.
It's one of the world's greatest sources of hydro-electric power, which in turn is also one of the reasons why it is no longer one of the worlds greatest sources of salmon.
Win some, lose some I guess.

The most important thing to me though was the fact that the river marked the boundary between Oregon and Washington.
I was at the doorstep of the final state in my walk, and from here, after having walked 3,540km I only had about 800km to go before reaching Canada!

My first stop of course, was a diner.
The two ladies at the adjoining table wanted to know if I'd been, "spending some time in the woods", and became quite animated when I told them just how much time I *had* been spending there.
I left the diner after being made to promise that I would send them a postcard when I finally made it to Canada.
I added Virginia and Margaret to my list.
My next priority was to pick up my supply parcel and make use of the

local laundromat.

Once having attended to that and deciding to spend the rest of the day and the night here, I wandered off to sort out a convenient place to pitch my tent.

There was a designated campground complete with shower and lavatory facilities on the river bank and close to town, but although the campground was generously free to long distance hikers I had my eyes on another location.

Not far from the ground and joined to the mainland by a small bridgeway, was a large and interesting looking wooded island.

I wasn't too sure whether or not it was legal to camp here, I suspected not, but it was a secluded and far more attractive spot than the sterile designated area. So just on dusk, I unobtrusively made my way onto the island and retired for the night out of sight and with a, "pound seat" view of the river traffic.

I drifted off into a contented sleep.

Stand by Washington, here I come...

Chapter Nine
Washington

Snoqualmie Pass, Stehekin - I meet my double, and Border

Marker 78

U p at first light and bulging with two, "All American" breakfasts, I made my way to appraoch the densely girdered, "Bridge of the Gods" that spans the Columbia River.

I paused at the bridge toll booth and spoke to the lady attendant, "I want to get across to Washington, do I have to pay anything?"

She smiled, "Well there's supposed to be a toll charge, but I'll let you across without paying."

The touch of kindness lifted some of the weight off my pack and I crossed to turn eastwards towards the small town of Stevenson where I hoped to buy some materials to fix my tent.

The zips on the outer fly of my tent were by now totally stuffed, and put mildly, I was getting a bit pissed off with the amounts of wind and rain that were joining me inside.

There was no way I was going to be able to get the zips replaced, so reaching Stevenson I hunted down a drapery/sewing store to buy sufficient lengths of velcro tape that would allow me to hermetically seal myself inside.

Even at the best of times entering these female domains makes me slightly uneasy, but after months of roughing it outside, the sudden gentile domesticity of the store made me feel a bit like the intrusive Bull in a China Shop, and the slightly bemused matron behind the counter watched as I sat on the ground outside her store, gluing and stitching the tape to a billowing tent.

As The Gimp would say, "George Spearing's Hook n' Groove Tape...Will hold anything...well almost anything...conditions apply."

My next supply parcel was at White Pass, which by the PCT proper was 236 kms away.

A look at my maps however, disclosed an alternative route that started at Stevenson, passing through the even smaller near-by settlement of Carson then bridging the 60 metre deep Wind River gorge to eventually meet up again with the PCT at the eastern end of Warren Gap near Panther Creek.

This alternative appealed to me, because besides the fact that I was already at Stevenson, it cut out an unattractive 21 mile loop that represented an extra day's walk.

I stopped briefly when I reached Carson to mail off a postcard to Uncle George reminding him *that I still hadn't given up,* and as I entered the store come post office, my ears pricked up when I overheard a couple of the locals discussing rattlesnakes.

"Yeah, been a lot of them around this year. I've killed off three or four of 'em."

Two things struck me about this conversation.

One was the casual way they talked about the snakes as if they were no more than a mouse nuisance or a plague of flies about the place.

I somehow couldn't imagine me old Mum who had lived in suburban Swansea in South Wales leaning across the garden fence and discussing them in quite the same way.

"Oh yes Gwyneth, real nuisance this year they are, lying around all over the place and waking me up with their rattling and what not. I'll just have to pop down to Tesco's and get something for them - I blame it all on the weather."

The other thing that struck me was my reaction to the comments. At the beginning of this journey I would have heartily joined in with an extermination programme, but now I suddenly realized I felt quite sorry for the poor serpents, and hoped that the day would never come when they were exterminated for good.

There are a few humans scattered around the planet that are far more qualified for that kind of treatment.

I arrived at Panther Creek early that evening and discovered that a slight detour got me to a designated campground near the edge of the creek.

"Normally charge $5", I was informed by the ground attendant, "but saying as you've walked so far you can pitch your tent for free."

I thanked him and walked through the ground to pitch my tent in the trees on the outer edge of the camp.

Passing some family groups, I was reminded of the strong patriotism that many Americans seem to have for their country.

A couple of separate families had driven in to set up camp and one of the first things they had done was to erect the Stars and Stripes outside their tent.

I'd noted that it was quite common to see houses in suburban America flying the national flag in their gardens and pondered the fact that a large percentage of Kiwis probably couldn't even describe their flag accurately, let alone think of taking it on a camping trip.

I don't think that they have any less patriotism. Just a different attitude.

As I left the attendant at the dusty road entrance, a police patrol car had cruised down through the trees.

Perched porkily on its dashboard beside the young cop, was a large stuffed pig!

The man has a sense of humour!

I awoke the next morning to discover that the rain was back, and in between showers quickly got a pot of porridge down me and broke camp.

Fording Panther Creek, the trail began a steep zigzag up through the trees in the direction of Big Huckleberry Mountain which peaked out

219

modestly at just over 4000ft.

A couple of hours later, heading up through the drizzle, I overtook a man and his young son of about ten. They were soaked through, looking cold and totally under-equipped.

Dressed in old jeans, thin cotton jackets, soft shoes and not much else, they looked like they shouldn't have been there.

They didn't look too affluent and the man carried an old small tattered day pack that appeared to be just about empty.

We exchanged the usual questions and answers and the man became quite enthusiastic, "Did you hear that son?! This man's just walked all the way from Mexico!"

The poor lad just stood there miserably, looking like he couldn't have given a toss if I'd just walked on the Moon.

I felt sorry for them and was a bit concerned for their well-being. I got the impression that the guy was trying to give his son the great outdoor experience, but wasn't quite up to it.

They were branching off in the opposite direction to me and the man mentioned some valley that wasn't on my map.

I wished them well and deciding that I could part with some of my supplies, asked them if they had enough food.

He cheerfully assured me that they did and waved as he disappeared through the rain, the boy miserably trailing along behind him.

I took a liking to the guy who had an amiable way about him and was enthusiastic enough, but at the risk of sounding heartless, I got the feeling that he was one of life's unlucky losers trying to do his best.

I hope it turned out to be a good experience for them both.

Progressing northwards through a mixed forest of Douglas fir, western hemlock and white pine I contoured around the edge of a recent lava flow (give or take a few thousand years) and eventually found myself at the southern end of Indian Heaven Wilderness and walking the crest of elongated Berry Mountain.

Mount St.Helens and Mount Adams lay ahead of me to the northwest and northeast and looking back I could see the elusive top of Mount Hood, a pleasure that had been denied me when I'd miserably traversed its lower slopes in the rain a week ago.

A legend of the Multnomah Indians of northwest Oregon embroils these three mountains in the old eternal triangle...Mt. St.Helens, the newly arrived squaw mountain and Wyeast (Mt.Hood) had fallen in love.

Unfortunately Klickitat (Mt.Adams) took a fancy to her as well, and Klickitat won the ensuing punch-up, forcing her to stay with him.

The young squaw mountain was having no hanky-panky though and after many years of forced abstinence, Klickitat's flames of passion died and both mountains became dormant.

The Multnomah have no doubt modified the legend since her spectacular eruption back in 1980!

I camped the night at clear watered Blue Lake tucked away at the northeast foot of Gifford Peak, and noted that the nights seemed to be getting a bit cooler now.

I was glad that the higher altitudes of the Sierra Nevada were now well and truly behind me, and I lay back in my camp revelling in the idyllic solitude.

A half-hearted attempt at catching some trout produced no results, so I crawled into my tent with a pot of re-hydrated Louisiana beans and dolefully considered perking them up with some of the failed salmon egg fish bait.

I could have used some of old Vern's angling expertise.

The following day was clear and warm and I pushed on through Gifford Pinchot National Forest to leave the Indian Heaven Wilderness at a point north of Sawtooth Mountain, eventually beginning an easy ascent to pass between the adjacent cinder cones of Twin Buttes.

There had been some brief excitement just before reaching

Sawtooth Mountain, when I'd passed a couple of horseriders heading in the opposite direction.

I was not exactly enamoured with horses after seeing what they tended to do to drinking water, but I stood well to one side and smiled amiably as the first horse sidled past me with no problem.

The second one was having none of it though. At the sight of me the horse went ballistic and started rising up, violently shying away from me as if I were some kind of Wilderness Horse Molester.

The rider struggled to gain control and only succeeded after I retreated and he'd sustained a battering from the trees at the side of the trail.

I'd heard of this kind of reaction before - apparently, with a large pack on your back a hiker can look a little less than human to a jittery horse and they tend to spin out.

Ha! Take *that* my four legged friend, and if your thinking of dumping in my water supply, I'll come and monster you some more!

I took advantage of this diversion to pause and study my map. Maybe I'd been on the trail too long.

The more I looked at the contour lines forming the cones of Twin Buttes, the more they looked like the cups of a magnificent D size brassiere that was more deserving of the name Twin Beauts!

If my topographic map had been a Rorschach ink blot test, then the psych would have been having a field day! As one patient said after sitting such a test and being told that he had a problem,

"It ain't my fault doc. You're the one who keeps showing me the dirty pictures!"

Towards the end of the 40km day, I descended to cross road 23 and meet up with the trailhead that led into the Mt. Adams Wilderness area.

It was here that I had my next close encounter with more four legged trail users, only this time there was no theatricals - each set of four legs dangled from the corners of a llama.

Five animals in all led by a packer and his clients. The llama train looked incongruous in that western setting, but they were certainly placid enough and apparently make excellent pack animals for rough terrain.

Somehow though, it just wouldn't be the same if Clint and The Duke rode a llama into the sunset.

I stopped briefly to talk with the packer and he told me that it had snowed 10 kms ahead last night.

He reckoned that we might be in for an early fall and I'd end up fighting snow by the time I reached the Canadian border.

I didn't want to hear stuff like that and hoping he was wrong, plodded off to camp just over a mile further on.

I'd dropped down into a small clearing amongst the trees that looked like a good camp spot, flipped off my pack and was in the process of taking a pee when a movement on the ground to my right caught my eye.

Snake!

What brand it was I don't know, it wasn't a rattler, but my finely tuned reflexes had me quickly side-stepping to the left, the unidentified snake slithering off rapidly to the right, and the hapless trouser-snake now left exposed to the vagaries of fate, rapidly counter-sinking itself like a tortoise's head ducking for cover, and giving me a soaking.

I hate it when that happens.

On the subject of bodily functions. There was a phenomenon I'd discovered on my walk that didn't seem to be covered in hiking manuals.

It concerned bladder control, and after much contemplation I've developed a theory on it that I call Spearing's Fundamental Law of Hiking.

The Law states, that bladder control is inversely proportional to Distance And Time Hiked Alone.

Known by the acronym D.A.T.H.A., it is responsible for the

223

DATHA EFFECT.

Earlier on in my walk, The Gimp who was no newcomer to long distance hiking had made the observation, "Man! When a hikers' gotta go he's really gotta go!"

I hadn't really considered the matter at the time, but as the months progressed I began to see what he meant - it was due to the DATHA effect.

This is how it works;

In normal society, one controls the urgencies of bladder emptying until a suitably private and convenient location has been found - thus constantly training the muscles that hold the bladder in check.

Lone hikers on the other hand have no such restrictions. Wherever they happen to be at any given time is always a private and generally convenient location, and emptying the bladder can be taken care of immediately with hardly a break in pace.

This means that the muscles concerned in bladder control are constantly being *unused*.

Do this daily for months on end and you suddenly notice a certain inability to, "hold on" when the occasion arises!

The DATHA Effect!

Not a lot of people know that.

I was up and at it before first light the next morning, the llama packer's forebodings of early snow near the Canadian border goading me into an earlier than usual start.

I figured that I was going to have to make the most of each day now to gain as much mileage as possible.

I needn't have bothered, because my longer day didn't gain me the desired progress.

Like an idiot I ended up going in the wrong direction, and on my fourth day into Washington temporarily misplaced myself again.

Head down and bum up I'd been making fast mileage, when it dawned on me that I seemed to be fording a lot of icy mountain run-offs that from memory weren't supposed to be there.

I was making such good progress that I couldn't be bothered stopping to retrieve the maps from my pack to do a check of my position and convinced myself that the creeks I was fording weren't usually on the map, and so that was why they weren't marked.

Tracking across snow and fording further substantial icy creeks, I eventually had to face the fact that I just might be going the wrong way. I stopped for a break, got my maps out and discovered that I'd wasted over half a day passing along the wrong side of Mt. Adams!

A glacier loomed off to my left, a steep drop off to a valley on my right. I studied my map... BOLLOCKS!!

Any glaciers should have been on my right, and according to my map it looked like the glacier I was below was Avalanche Glacier which was in the opposite direction to where I should have been.

I was on the wrong side of the frigging mountain!!

I stormed off, retracing my steps, wasting valuable time, energy and food, hurling abuse at the map, the mountain, the trail, America, and eventually at the right culprit - myself.

How the hell can you go the wrong way round a 12,688ft white lump like Mt. Adams?!

I shouldn't have been allowed out. DAMN!!

I eventually got myself relocated and after hiking through some beautiful scenery with Mt.Adams awesomely and tidily ensconced on my *right hand* side, forded Killen Creek and made camp in a better frame of mind near the Highline trail that led eastwards to the Yakima Indian reservation.

I hadn't seen much in the way of Indians, Yakima or otherwise, except for a solitary middle-aged Indian woman gathering huckleberries.

I'd called out a greeting to her as I passed but she'd either chosen to ignore me or hadn't heard me, so rather than risk upsetting her I carried on and left her uninterrupted.

My last camp before White Pass was at Walput creek, 39 kms further on in the Goat Rocks Wilderness area and still paralleling the western flanks of the Yakima reservation.

I would eventually enter only briefly into this Indian land before leaving it a mile or so later at Cispus Pass.

I sat contentedly by the side of the creek listening to its voices and studying the snowy peak of Mt.Adams.

This hearing of voices was one strange wilderness phenomenon that had me stopping in my tracks the first time I heard them.

The, "voices" always appeared to be in the mid distance and not quite intelligible.

I'd thought that I must be starting to lose it at first, but soon realized that what caused them was the wind in trees or equipment resonating at a frequency close to that of the human voice.

The gurgling and splashing of creeks and rivers could also come up with some quite human-like sounds, and like Walput Creek, could prove to be rather entertaining.

It was quite uncanny.

After experiencing the snowbound High Sierras, most of the passes in Oregon and Washington were a bit of an anti-climax in comparison and although snow patched, Cispus Pass at 6460ft was no exception.

Truth be known, I was quite contented that subsequent passes tended towards the anti side of climax, and hopefully looked forward to a leisurely stroll into Canada.

Dropping down and fording the two small tributaries of the Cispus River, I eventually climbed to the western slopes of Old Snowy Mountain and then traversed the upper slopes of Packwood Glacier at 7080ft, leaving the trail's highest point in Washington.

Tieton Pass at 4570ft (1393m) was the last milestone before reaching White Pass at Highway 12.

It was here that I met up with Alison and her dog Shame, and we hiked the remaining 18 kms to the highway together.
I asked her how her dog got a name like Shame but she looked a little embarrassed at that, and said that she didn't know really. I'm sure there was a story there, but if there was, Alison wasn't telling.
Alison was good company with a lively sense of humour.

Originally from Arizona, she now lived in Portland Oregon and was up in the backwoods of Washington doing a few hikes.
She was in her early twenties, attractive, well travelled, very secure and not a bit worried about treading these isolated spots alone.
"My folks worry about me getting attacked or something out here, but I tell them there's more chance of running into trouble back in the towns and cities. Most people you find out here in these kind of places are one hundred percent."

I had to agree with her there, but hoped that one day she didn't meet up with an exception that broke the rule.

We dropped down off Hogback Mountain along its northeast ridge. I'd hoped to get views of Mount Rainier that I'd be reaching in a few days time, but the weather had packed in again and all I got was grey. I mused to myself that Mount *Rainier* probably would be.

Descending steeply and parallel with a ski lift, we finally crossed the highway to check that Alison's car was still okay and to head for the village's restaurant for a decent meal.
Shame waited obediently outside while we hit the trough and were unwittingly entertained by a middle aged be-jewelled matron at an adjoining table.
She was into a loud monologue on her packaged tour adventures through some third world country.

"....And it was just *terrible* to see how they lived (pass the mayo and the fries honey)...next year I'm gonna do Egypt."

We pitched our tents in darkness near a horse corral, and after a wet night in which I discovered at 3am that I'd set up in a natural rain run-off, we packed up and returned to the restaurant for breakfast.
Alison had looked at my wet sleeping bag as I stuffed it into my pack, "Why didn't you come in with me and share my tent?"
A pleasant thought, but I'm sure that at three in the morning, Shame would have considered me to be on his attack list if I'd started knocking on tent doors!

I loaded up with the supply parcel that had arrived at the post office and we said our goodbyes. Alison climbed into her car and headed south for Portland, whilst I climbed into my boots and headed north into the William O. Douglas Wilderness and towards the village that lay five days away at Snoqualmie Pass.

The Cascade Range of Oregon and so far most of Washington, was proving to be much easier terrain, and I was averaging at least 32 kms a day. Elevations were a lot lower which of course meant less likely problems from snow, so most of the time the trail was a lot easier to follow. The exceptions, and this trail was full of exceptions, were some of the logged areas. They posed problems obstacle-wise and at times had me clambering like an ungainly and highly pissed off beetle over debris and fallen trees.
Re-locating your bearings and finding the trail became quite a game after crossing areas like these.

The rain and drizzle that now seemed to be the trend stubbornly followed me through Chinook Pass, and I took advantage of a weather break to make an early camp in mid afternoon at Sheep Lake.
The following day was the first of September and was heralded by the welcome return of the sun, albeit accompanied by a chilly wind that reminded me that winter was waiting in the wings.

Throwing the usual pot of porridge down my throat I set off for my next campsite at Government Meadows. This section of the trail taking me into the Norse Peak Wilderness was once the attraction for gold and silver prospectors and they had left their mark on points along the way with evocative names like Sourdough Gap, Pickhandle Gap and Bullion Pass.

I was always conscious of the fact that many of the areas I was passing through must still hold gold deposits, and my Scottish genes encouraged a subconscious watch for any tell-tale glitter of the elusive yellow metal.

The nearest I'd come to striking gold was further south in California when I'd been crossing a creek. I was about to climb up out of it when I noticed hundreds of little golden flecks shining up from the sandy bottom!

Deciding that I would probably never have to return to work again, I excitedly scooped up handfuls of the bottom. I don't know what sort of mineral the flecks were, but on bringing them to the surface they turned a depressing grey/silver sort of colour with very little body to them.

Unfortunately, it was a trick of light reflection that had produced the seductive colour and had momentarily provided a fool with some gold!

Descending through silver fir and western hemlock, I crossed Louisiana Saddle and dropped lower again to reach Government Meadow. I'd decided to carry on a bit further than here but came to a halt, when showing through the trees was the outline of an old derelict cabin.

It proved to be too much of an attraction for me, and it ended up becoming my home for the night.

Above its doorless doorway, someone had nailed a poetic sign warning that the ghost of a Mike Urich would deal to anyone who harmed the trees around there. Luckily my only arboreal transgression had been a lot further south when I'd carved Sadie's name into a tree during a moment of romantic weakness.

The spooky Mike in question was apparently a dedicated trail worker from the forties.

The cabin was a gloomy shambles inside, with dirt floor and an almost unserviceable wood-burning stove. As night fell it looked just the place for a ghostly visitation. Fortunately the only visitation that I did have, was from a rough looking crew that consisted of a father, his two sons in their early twenties and a girlfriend.

They'd driven a four wheel drive into the area somewhere nearby and were having a look around. One of the first things the father said after greeting me was, "We're the ones who trash things around here!" I didn't doubt him.

The two boys didn't say much at all, and looked on vacantly as the girl did all the talking,

"What you doin' livin' in this old cabin way out here all on your own?" I tried to explain that I was just passing through and that I didn't really live there all the time but I don't think it sank in.

She smiled up at me, "Ain't he got the nicest accent? Ah could just listen to him all day!

What you need is a woman to look after you."

I glanced at the two boys who stood there looking like their brains were hurting, and hoped that they weren't slowly processing a conclusion that I might be a rival that needed eliminating.

They eventually left me to the business of cooking up some tucker, and as I sat outside the cabin eating my dinner in the solitary peacefulness of the woods with the shadows slowly lengthening. I happily contemplated that this might not be such a bad place to live.

The only other people I was to come across before reaching Snoqualmie, were a couple of bear hunters who seemed genuinely impressed with my journey and the fact that the trail they were standing on led all the way down to Mexico.

"Jeez! I'd heard the trail goes all the way south! So it really does huh?!" They gave me some chocolate sachets, coffee granules and granola bars and asked if I'd seen any bear in the area - I truthfully replied that I had not.

I then felt a bit guilty when they asked if I'd seen any deer. I had, but I replied in the negative. When I thought of my four-legged buddy all the way back at Moosehead Creek, I didn't feel like helping them to wipe out any of her kind.

It took me over 45 kms to reach Snoqualmie the next day after getting confused in one of the logged-over areas. By the time I'd sorted myself out I'd added at least another 6 kms of unnecessary travel. I was beginning to dislike loggers, not for what they did to the trees but for what they did to my feet and peace of mind.

I stood high on a ridge looking down at the village far below, Interstate 90 threaded itself through it and behind the various buildings stood the impressively craggy peaks of the Alpine Lakes Wilderness that was to be the next stage of my journey. I headed down the steep incline to the village and just before getting there, caught myself unconsciously finger-combing my beard and hair and tidying up the tattered bandanna that was tied around my neck.

This amused me and took me years back to the Saturday morning movies of my childhood.

There was always a scene where the rag-tag band of cowboys would appear on the edge of town and before entering the delights of civilization, would smooth down their matted hair to improve their chances - the fact that they still looked like an unwashed bag of crap no matter what they did to improve their appearance didn't seem to occur to them.

Maybe this was a natural human reaction after all, and not just a figment of the script writers imagination!

It was early evening when I reached the village, and as the place had a good feel to it I decided to take some time out and spend a couple of nights here.

I booked in at the Wardholm B&B and after eating at the local diner, set about discovering what a bed felt like again.

It was bliss!

Brett and Brian, a couple of southbound hikers, were also in residence and despite Brett's striking similarity to Charles Manson, they both turned out to be amicable guys.

Some days back, I'd snapped the handle off my plastic spoon which was my only eating/cooking utensil.

I'd experimented with a couple of twigs as chopsticks before finally carving a spoon out of a bit of tree. I was quite proud of this effort but it wasn't quite as efficient as the real thing. So I was appreciative when Brian kindly presented me with a spare spoon that they carried.

We also discussed trail conditions, and I was glad to hear that they hadn't struck too much in the way of snow further north.

They intended heading all the way south through the Sierras and I thought that they might be pushing their luck by leaving it a bit late. By the time they got there it would be moving a bit close to winter with the chance of getting caught in some heavy snow falls.

Maybe they got lucky.

The next day after laundering some of the trail dirt out of my gear, I checked in at the post office to pick up my supply parcel from Trail Foods and also a surprise package from New Zealand.

I sat in the sun outside and opened up my mail. John Tuke had tuned in to my needs and unprompted had sent me on a replacement pair of hiking shorts.

The guy must have been a mind reader as my current pair had been shredded and patched up several times by now and I was in extreme danger of breaching the decency laws of the state of Washington at any moment.

He'd also enclosed a copy of the Auckland Herald to get me up to speed on the latest Kiwi news. Making the headlines was the tragic story of a group of climbers on Mount Ruapehu who had been caught out in atrocious snow conditions with the result that some had subsequently perished.

One of the prominent members of the successful search and rescue party had been an American ski instructor in New Zealand on a working holiday.

I finished reading the paper and disappeared into the diner to work on my fat reserves.

The waitress put down my plate, "Where are you from?", she asked.

"New Zealand."

Her face brightened, "My boyfriend's over in New Zealand. He's got a job as a ski instructor and has just been helping out in a search and rescue on one of the mountains down there."

A bell rang in my head and I asked her what his name was.

Sure enough it was the same guy mentioned in the newspaper article. I presented her with the paper and she went away a very delighted waitress!

This was really quite uncanny and I pondered the odds of John sending me a newspaper *unsolicited* to this *particular* town and then being served by that *particular* waitress!

John had also been instrumental in my coincidental meeting with old Mountain Goat Vern high up in the remote Sierra Nevada.

Maybe he should trade firefighting for a career in clairvoyance or something.

The next section of my journey was going to be quite a long one. About 274 kms to the small mountain settlement of Stehekin where I would re-supply once again for the final time.

I left at 0700, farewelling Peg and Bob the owners of the B&B, and climbing steadily away from Snoqualmie to head for Chikamin Pass, eventually making a 2000ft (610m) steeply switchbacked descent to cross Delate Creek and camp for the night.

The views along this section were well worth the grunt they entailed and went a long way to providing a panacea for the 2200ft climb that followed, taking me to the top of Escondido Ridge.

The northern Cascades stretch in a plunging, climbing, serrated mass that boasts 750 glaciers all the way from Snoqualmie to the Canadian border.

From the ascent and from working my way along the ridge, I could see a maze of mountains and valleys all around me, Lemah Mountain, Waptus Lake, Mt.Stuart, all adding their presence to the kaleidoscope of alpine scenery.

Suddenly movement at the head of the valley way below me caught my eye, I focused on the rapidly moving object and spotted a jet fighter, flying low and hugging the mountainous terrain. It passed below me, reaching the end of the valley and banking steeply to disappear up over the mountain and down into the next valley.

The pilot's skill was impressive - move over Tom Cruise!

This was the second time I'd been surprised by a 'plane. The first time had been back in California, when a huge black jet engined transport or troop carrier had suddenly loomed up over the ridge above me, passed low overhead and disappeared towards the horizon on a ground hugging course.

Excellent country to train in. No one to bother except the odd nutter wandering around!

Iraq was rattling its sabres at the time and I wondered if the low flying aerial activity was a bit of radar evasion training.

After a 25 mile day finished off with a long hot climb to Deep Lake lying at the southern reaches of the Wenatchee Forest I was glad to dump the weight off my back and kick back. The old body was showing cumulative signs of wear.

234

I'd lost a lot of weight as well as a toenail on each foot. The nerve endings in my toes and the balls of my feet were completely dead and had no feeling, which given the use they were getting was probably a good thing.

However, I noted too that my upper thighs near the hip had gone dead (probably from pack weight pressing on nerves) and I hoped that this numbness wouldn't spread laterally to more social areas.

A man's gotta do what a man's gotta do, but there are some things that require a little feeling!

To compound my bodily woes, I'd also badly bruised my right hip in a fall whilst fording a river. My acrobatic leaps from boulder to boulder had finally caught up with me and I'd come in for a slippery landing, skidding off and coming down on my hip with the combined weight of myself and my pack.

I'd rolled through the water to drag myself up and lie on the bank building character and hoping that I hadn't broken anything.

Luckily I hadn't, and after a brief rest had been able to painfully get on the move again. Added to all this was the recurring problem of painful shinsplints that seemed to mysteriously come and go.

My tent was also showing the rigours of the journey. The velcro that I'd replaced the zips on the outer fly with at Stevenson was still doing an admirable job of sealing me off from the elements, and in many ways was better than the original zips.

A new problem however, had been the zips on the inner mesh flap that had by now also packed up. Because of the taut semi-circular shape of the flap, I was unable to glue and stitch Velcro tape successfully. This meant that the inner compartment and I had become accessible to rodents, and on some nights I'd been awoken by mice, "line dancing" over my face and chest.

They were tenacious little sods, and no amount of bellowing and thumping seemed to deter them for long. I finally managed to alleviate the problem by attaching several strings to the flap and tying them up to partially seal off any large inviting openings, hopefully lessening the chance of ingesting a rodent in my sleep!

I'd pitched my modified tent amongst the trees and was sitting outside writing up the day's progress when a sound had me looking up. About ten metres away, an old character who must have been close to seventy, was making his way past my camp, totally unaware of my presence.

Dressed in old denims, with a bow-legged gait, hunched over back and scraggly white beard, he looked like an apparition from the old mining west.

He carried a water canteen in his hand and was obviously headed for the nearby creek.

"G'day!"

He spun round, scratching at his beard, head thrust forward and peering in my direction.

A Gabby Hayes clone.

"Hi, didn't see yuh there!"

He ambled over and we got talking. I was impressed to hear that he and his mate, another old-timer, had ridden in on horseback to spend some time in the woods.

They now lived in Spokane, but had worked extensively on ranches during their youth.

He in turn was impressed with my story, and slapped his thigh enthusiastically when I told him where I'd started out from, "Goldarn it! Ain't many *young* fellers could do that!"

I mentally noted his emphasis on the word young, and thought if *he* thinks I'm old, then this trip has been harder on me than I realized!

In retrospect though, I guess that being closer to fifty than forty, I was a bit past the egg stage and consoled myself with the old adage that, "You're only as old as you feel." Or as one of the troops at work had once told me with a grin, "You're only as old as *the women* you feel!"

I dwelt briefly on this, and mused dolefully to myself that considering the severance of relations with the irate Sadie, that particular adage wasn't going to apply to me for quite a while.

"What time are yuh leavin' in the mornin'?"

I told him that I usually start to move out at about first light.

"Well, I'll see yuh then - I'm comin' over to see how yuh get all that stuff on your back!"

Sure enough, he appeared through the trees right on daybreak and watched fascinated as I broke camp and hefted my pack up onto my back.

We shook hands, wished each other well, and I ambled off down the trail.

I looked back just before disappearing from sight, and he was still there, peering after me and giving a final wave.

His enthusiasm for what I was doing gave my morale a megaton boost, and not for the first time on this journey, the strength of someone elses spirit had raised mine.

Once more my pack became weightless. Long may he saddle-up before finally riding off into the sunset.

This area of Washington was out of a picture book; mountains, meadows, lakes. Indian Pass, Fire Creek Pass, Mica Lake and the long endless climb up to Miner's Creek.

The perfect reflection in the partially frozen Mica Lake that fed Milk Creek 2000ft below provided a photograph that was almost impossible to determine which way was up.

Country straight off a chocolate box lid!

Suiattle Pass at just under 6000ft was my last pass before Stehekin, and after reaching it I studied my maps and again decided to deviate slightly from the Crest trail. An old trail branched off to the north, closely following the South Fork of Agnes Creek.

Besides keeping me closer to water supplies which is always a

237

comfort, the contour lines on my map showed a relatively straight and easy mainly downhill run all the way to the Stehekin turn-off at High Bridge.

Apparently this old trail was unmaintained, but the route looked okay to me, and in the event turned out to be a pleasant detour and the scene of an intriguing meeting.

Agnes Creek flowed through a picturesque canyon and gorge that cut its way through the Wenatchee Forest in the Glacier Peak Wilderness. The canyon rivalled some of the finer locations in the Sierra Nevada further south, and bore enough tree and plant species to satisfy a whole thicket of David Bellamy's - Western white pine, Engelmann spruce, western hemlock, Douglas fir and western red cedar were but a few of the species that I could now blithely roll off my tongue at the drop of a botanist.

I was enjoying myself, and rapt that Canada was now within comparative spitting distance.

I looked up to see a rather dishevelled figure approaching me. We both came to a halt a few feet from each other and I wondered why he had such a surprised look on his face.

"What are you doing here?!!"

I thought about that, and decided that as everybody had to be *somewhere,* then that was a somewhat irrational question.

"What do you mean?"

"I passed you yesterday, you was going in the opposite direction to me and heading for Stehekin!"

"No I wasn't, yesterday I was twenty miles south of here."

He shook his head incredulously, "Well I tell yuh buddy, you got a double. I could swear it's you I talked to!"

I finally convinced him that we hadn't met before and we went our separate ways.

I put the guys confusion down to some of the plant life he'd been smoking.

238

The intrigue hadn't finished yet though, and a few hundred metres from the Stehekin trail turn-off I was greeted by another hiker.

"Hi George!"

I was taken aback that this complete stranger knew my name. My God! I was world famous!

His greeting was immediately followed by an apology, "Oh sorry. I thought you were someone else from Stehekin. You look like him!"

This was getting more and more interesting. This doppelganger whoever he was, even had the *same name* as me! I couldn't wait to meet up with him and see what I looked like!

Another interesting and more sobering feature at this point, was the sign requesting that any sightings of Grizzly bears be reported to a ranger. Old grizzly was one American I *didn't* want to meet up with!

The road into Stehekin ran for about 18 kms alongside the Stehekin River and started at a deserted ranger station. It took off in an easterly direction at right angles to my northerly course, and as I would have to return to this point to recommence my journey, I didn't much feel like hoofing it all the way in if I didn't have to.

I knew that a shuttle bus ran this road to the settlement, and incorrectly thinking that there was one due I settled down to wait outside the ranger station.

A small brightly coloured snake slithered obligingly across the open gravelly ground in front of me. Thinking he'd make a good photo, I attempted to slow up his progress by turning him around with my boot, in between making frantic dashes back to my pack to try and disinter my camera from its recesses.

The little fellow had a surprising turn of speed, and I was in the midst of one of these frenetic dashes between snake and pack when a vehicle pulled up.

The driver grinned out the window, "Getting a bit of exercise? Hiking not enough for yuh huh?!"

The relieved serpent took advantage of the diversion and made a safe uninterrupted dash for freedom, his opportunity for stardom gone forever.

I sheepishly explained what I'd been up to and then accepted his offer of a lift, the shuttle bus wasn't due for another three hours.

I finally reached my last pick-up point before Canada.

Stehekin, an Indian name meaning, "The way through", must be one of the most isolated communities in America.

There were about sixty people living there.

The only way in is either on foot through the mountains, or by boat or float plane, to land on the river.

They had no telephone and radio communication was limited by the surrounding mountains.

They have a horse packer station, a post office, a few small stores, a "log cabin" type school for the junior kids, a restaurant and that's about it.

Because of their isolation, I was told that children at Stehekin can legally leave school at the age of twelve.

I wandered down the road, sussing likely spots to pitch a tent and get some food.

There standing in the middle of the road talking to a female ranger, was presumably my hiking lookalike!

I stepped up and introduced myself as a kindred spirit.

The ranger smiled, "Hey you two guys could be brothers!"

I told them of my experiences with the others who had thought the same, and added, not altogether untruthfully, "I'm a bit disappointed, I thought I was better looking than that."

As Robbie Burns once muttered, "Oh would some power the giftie gie us, to see oursel's as others see us!

George Woodard, a semi-retired railroad employee, took the comment in good humour, and I enjoyed his company for the next day or so before he pulled out ahead of me, heading for the Canadian border.

He'd done about 900 kms on the trail, and like myself, preferred hiking alone. Especially for the final leg.

From what he told me, he seemed to spend about half of the year instructing crews in Boston railroad marshalling yards, and the other half on the move through wilderness areas - seemed like a good system to me.

I met up with him for the final time in the Manning Park Lodge in Canada, and we shared a bit of luxury accommodation before heading our separate ways.

I left this community with mixed feelings, I had only about 130km to go to reach Canada.

It would be great to finish but it would also mean the finish of what had become my way of life.

Many thoughts passed through my head. What if I sustained an injury and couldn't reach the border after so many miles of travel? What if the weather changed and I got snowed in?

My goal was so close that fear of failure at the eleventh hour was making me paranoid!

After leaving a letter care of the post office for Ziggy and The Gimp who were still somewhere further south, I boarded the small shuttle and was back on the trail by 0830.

The weather was excellent, very hot with no signs of the snowfall that I knew could not be too far away.

I bowled blissfully along thinking of all the comforts of civilization that were awaiting me at the end of the walk, when a sudden crashing noise stopped me dead in my tracks.

I knew that noise!

A creek lay somewhere below me to my left. The undergrowth and tree-covered ground to my right rose in an incline. It was from somewhere just above me that the noise had emanated... Silence.

I started walking again and minutes later I was halted by more heavy rustling of undergrowth.

My adrenalin-swamped brain leapt frantically about in my skull, leaping up at alcoves and pulling out information concerning grizzlies stalking their prey and festooning bits and pieces of hikers across the landscape.

I spoke severely to my brain and told it to stop being silly and calm down, but it insisted in leaping around pulling out more and more unsettling information and screaming, "What do *you* know! Who d'you think you are? *Davey bloody Crockett?!!*"

The bear that had been causing all this excitement suddenly emerged into a small clearing about 10 metres above me.

He stopped, sniffed at the air and swung his head around to look at me. I noted with some consolation that there didn't seem to be any sign of a hump on his back, and if I'd got it right, that at least meant that he wasn't a grizzly.

To my eyes though, the hairy sod was big enough to be whatever he wanted to be.

With a low growl and to a relief of proportions that you have no idea of, he swung away from me and lumbered off uphill at a great rate of knots.

The encounter had just about OD'd me on adrenalin, and my brain who moments before had been a gibbering cowardly wreck, was now strutting around informing anyone who would listen, that,"We sure scared that dumb bear off!", and "What a fantastic experience that was!"

I reminded him not to skite until we were sitting in a bus or a shopping mall or something, and continued watchfully on my way.

Thirty two kilometres from Stehekin, I stopped on the east side of Rainy Pass. Highway 20 cuts through this pass before swinging off on its paved way west, and according to my written information, a lay-by rest area for horse packers and hikers complete with, "plush" toilet facilities was available here.

Indeed there was, but the turn of a tap at the ablution block revealed that water was not part of the deal.

Bollocks! This was a problem. Although I'd passed by water on the way, I'd foregone the pleasures of filtering and carrying it, assuming that I'd have an abundance of the stuff here at Rainy Pass.

It was late in the day and I was totally knackered.

Even though I knew that if I carried on I would eventually meet up with some hopefully running creeks, I was mentally and physically just not prepared to do so. I cast around looking for some source of moisture and finally got lucky.

A gutter ran along the edge of the parking area, and along it trickled a smear of water. I spent about an hour painstakingly collecting it in my pot from whence I could filter it before I'd amassed enough to sufficiently re-hydrate my evening meal with enough left over to half fill my cup. I crouched there in the gutter like a disgruntled troll, muttering foul oaths and curses upon the heads of the Ablution Block Maintenance Men of America and their bureaucratic overlords.

If they're going to have a bog complete with friggin' taps in the middle of the wilderness, *why couldn't they make sure the bloody things work!*

Sorry guys, I get like that sometimes.

The following two days the weather deteriorated and I got as much water as I wanted, wandering along through alternate bouts of cloud, rain, drizzle and thunderclaps.

Visibility was down, and unfortunately I was denied some usually pleasant vistas. The inclement weather couldn't dampen my spirit now though - I was on the home run!

My colours nailed to the mast-head and telegraphs lashed to full ahead!

Cutthroat Pass, Methow Pass, Glacier Pass, Holman Pass; four days after leaving Stehekin, on September 17th two days short of five calender months, I left the Pasayten Wilderness of the United States and crossed into Canada at border marker 78 in the Okanogan Forest.

My triumphant entry into Canada wasn't without one last hiccup though.

I'd inadvertently extended my trip by managing to go off course about 10km before the border, veering to the east and climbing for about an hour before my brain snapped out of it, checked the map contours and realized that the border was not in an, "up" direction.

Wrong Way Spearing, true to the end.

Unwanted detours aside, I'd done it - 4280km from Mexico to Canada, and I'd walked every single step of the way!

I camped for the night next to an empty horse corral on Canadian soil in the Okanogan Forest, next morning hiking out the 11km to the highway at Manning Park.

Stopping off at the ranger tourist station to make an entry in the trail book, I overheard a conversation between one of the rangers and a couple of tourists.

He was telling them that if they drove their RV up to a particular point, and then walked in along a trail for a few hundred metres, they might just get lucky and see the marmot or two that they were hoping to sight.

I smiled to myself and couldn't help feeling a little smug.

For months now, those little creatures had been my immediate neighbours and confidantes.

Seen marmots?

I'd *dined and danced* with marmots!

Epilogue

My next couple of weeks would be spent assimilating the trappings of civilization again - vehicles, getting used to the strangely uncomfortable softness of a bed, the onslaught of advertising...and remembering that it is not generally acceptable to make eye contact with strangers that pass by.

But first, after a couple of days of the, "easy life" I decided it was time to announce my presence to the appropriate bureaucracy.

I boarded a greyhound for the nearest customs point which was some distance away in the town of Osoyoos, and eventually made my way up the road to once more approach the U.S./Canadian border.

The boundary between the Canadian and American checkpoints was a wide tarmacked sort of, "No mans land", and as I strolled across it out of Canada and towards the U.S., I could sense rather than see several pairs of eyes marking my progress.

Part of the deal for being allowed into the U.S. was that you had to inform them when you were leaving.

I was about to do my civic duty.

I opened the door to the U.S. building and was greeted by an unsmiling young customs officer standing directly in front of me, looking very sharp in uniform, close-cropped hair, gun at hip, and arms akimbo.

"Can we help you", unsmiling.

"Yeah, I've come to check out of the U.S."

He lifted one arm and pointed in turn to my pack, the corner of the room, and to the ground in front of him, "Why don't you take *that,* put it over *there,* and then come back *here.*"

"Oh,oh", I thought, "This one has the bureaucrat gene *and* a gun to back it up!"

I returned dutifully to the spot in front of him and repeated my intention.

He looked at me suspiciously, "You want to check out of the U.S.? I just saw you coming out of Canada."

This could get complicated, I hoped that his brain wouldn't get stuck. "That's because I left the U.S. a couple of days ago and entered Canada through the woods."

He looked at me as if I was Public Enemy No.1, "Why didn't you enter through a regular checkpoint?"

His somewhat threatening demeanour wasn't earning him any points, and I didn't feel like making it any easier for him.

"Because there wasn't one in the Pasayton Wilderness where I left the U.S."

"How did you get to the border?"

"I walked"

He gave me a look that said, "smart-ass". "Where did you walk from?"

I played my trump card, "The Mexican border, off-road."

A look of confusion flitted across his face, I think his brain was beginning to hurt.

He stared again at the immigration details in my passport, then called over and conferred with an older female colleague. She smiled briefly, "Unusual way of getting here, but his papers are all okay. Can't see any problem."

He looked a little disappointed, "You don't want to look in his pack or anything?"

She shook her head in the negative and turned away.

He silently and unsmilingly handed me back my passport and I re-crossed the tarmac to enter the Canadian checkpoint.

I was beginning to enjoy myself!

The atmosphere in the Canadian sector was completely different. No sign of any weapons, uniforms not quite as sharp, and a friendly greeting, "Hi."

"Hi, I've come to check into Canada."

He smiled, "I just saw you walk out of Canada."

Oh no, here we go again!

"Well I arrived in Canada a couple of days ago along the Pacific Crest trail at Manning Park and there wasn't a customs point there."

"Why didn't you check in at a Royal Canadian Mounted Police station then?"

"I didn't know you could do that. In any case, I didn't see any."

He smiled, "Ah well, I suppose there's no point in looking through your bag, you'd have got rid of all the drugs by now."

I joined in the game, "Yeah, smoked the last joint yesterday!"

He shunted me onto a colleague, where after a bit of computer punching and a credit check, I was given a six month entry permit, and returned to the bus station a bona fide and legal immigrant.

My, "unorthodox" entry into Canada had brought home to me how impossible it must be to completely control such a vast border. I guess custom points are for honest folk and villains that don't like getting mud on their boots! With the turn in world events, it must be quite a worry for the authorities concerned.

My next port of call was to be Saskatoon, where I'd spend a couple of weeks with good friends Leslie and Bob Lynch before leaving Canada. The bus left at about midnight that night, and that evening I was hunched down on a bench at the depot, killing time.

A young lad of about eleven or twelve who'd obviously been sent out to pick up a few groceries, approached me from out of a nearby general store. He stuck out his hand holding about a dollar in change, "I want you to have this."

I was taken aback, "No, I don't need that! You use it to buy yourself some sweets or something!"

He was insistent, "No, I really want you to have it."

There was no putting him off from his good Samaritan role, and I finally ended up reluctantly accepting it.

Although laundered and showered, I still sported my beard and trail clothes, and realized that to some folk I must look like a middle-aged guy down on my luck. I was touched by the lad's kind, albeit unnecessary concern for a stranger.

This was in direct contrast to the, "sprog from hell" that I was eventually confronted with on the overnight train to Toronto.

A family of two harassed parents and their hyperactive ankle-biter boarded the crowded train soon after Saskatoon and took the seats in front of me.

He had a toy police car complete with siren, that despite futile objections from his parents, he insisted on continuously demonstrating. My spirits dropped further as he directed his attentions to me, standing up on his seat and peering over the back at me, in between sticking his police car in his mother's ear and running it across his father's balding head.

I was wearing a T shirt that uncovered the tattoos on my arms, a legacy from my younger seafaring days. The demon child spotted these. "Are those pictures on your arms tattoos?", he demanded.

"Yes they're tattoos", I smiled. (please piss off now and leave me in peace you horrible little sod.)

"Are you a bad guy?"

"Yeah, I'm a bad guy." (maybe now he'd leave me alone.)

Wrong move.

He immediately turned around on his seat, faced down the carriage and began shrieking at the top of his voice, *There's a bad guy behind me! There's a bad guy behind me!"*

For the length of the carriage, heads turned to stare back at the monster that the dear child had disclosed.

I sat there with a sheepish grin on my face, trying desperately to look like a good guy.

The parents sat there and groaned - I sat there and wished I was back in the woods!

My journey through the States had become a milestone in my life, with a wide range of experiences. Notwithstanding demon children, surly customs officials, and postal clerks from hell, I was impressed by the spontaneity and kindness of the American people and by their country.

The walk had taken me five months.

It hadn't changed me in any major way, except maybe to bring home to me the insignificance of the individual in the overall scheme of things.

I read a slightly derogatory article sometime after my walk, that said long distance hiking was just escapism.

Well, I agree in part.

My walk made me realize that the brain, when called upon, prioritizes - and survival is a big fat number one in that rascals' list.

Hunger, thirst, and shelter fit nicely into the survival slot of your psyche, and long distance hikers are always hungry, thirsty, and continuously heading for a target that will afford some degree of safety and comfort at the end of the day.

The wind that is trying to blow you off a ridge, is also the same wind that blows away all those extraneous and niggling thoughts of workday decisions, personal relationships, leaking roofs and rust spots in your car.

So I agree it is a form of escapism, but it is an escape to a basic instinct that is rooted deeply in all living creatures, and it is a healthy escape.

One could argue, that modern day living with all its associated materialism is really the escapism.

Anyhow, I hadn't become more religious, more withdrawn or even more confident in my everyday doings.

But when the occasion arises, I *can* say, "Oh yeah, I've done a bit of hiking mate."

And even though by the end of the journey I'd lost 9.5kg in weight, I'd gained a million tons of satisfaction...and a lifetime of memories.

Thank you America, I owe you one!

US/Canadian Border

Pasayton Wilderness/Okanogan Forest, Marker 78

AREAS TRAVERSED

STATES

California, Oregon, Washington.

WILDERNESS AREAS

Hauser Wilderness, San Jacinto Wilderness, San Gorgonio Wilderness, Cucamonga Wilderness, San Gabriel Wilderness, Domeland Wilderness, Golden Trout Wilderness, John Muir Wilderness, Minarets Wilderness, Ansel Adams Wilderness, Hoover Wilderness, Emigrant Wilderness, Carson Iceberg Wilderness, Mokelumne Wilderness, Desolation Wilderness, Granite Chief Wilderness, Caribou Wilderness, Bucks Lake Wilderness, Castle Crags Wilderness, Trinity Alps Wilderness, Russian Wilderness, Marble Mountain Wilderness, Red Buttes Wilderness, Sky Lakes Wilderness, Mt.Thielson Wilderness, Diamond Peak Wilderness, Three Sisters Wilderness, Mount WashingtonWilderness, Mount Jefferson Wilderness, Mount Hood Wilderness, Columbia Wilderness, Indian Heaven Wilderness, Mount Adams Wilderness, Goat Rocks Wilderness, William O.Douglas Wilderness, Norse Peak Wilderness, Alpine Lakes Wilderness, Henry M. Jackson Wilderness, Glacier Peak Wilderness, Pasaytan Wilderness.

NATIONAL FORESTS

Cleveland National Forest, San Bernardino Nat Forest, Angeles National Forest, Sequoia National Forest, Inyo National Forest, Sierra National Forest, Toiyabe National Forest, Eldorado National Forest, Tahoe National Forest, Plumas National Forest, Lassen National Forest, Shasta-Trinity Nat Forest, Klamath National Forest, Rogue River Nat Forest, Winema National Forest, Umpqua National Forest, Deschutes National Forest, Willamette National Forest, Mount Hood National Forest, Gifford

Pinchot Nat Forest, Snoqualmie National Forest, Wenatchee National Forest, Mount Baker National Forest, Okanogan National Forest.

STATE PARKS

Cuyamaca Rancho State Park, Anza Borrega Desert State Park, Mt.San Jacinto State Park.

NATIONAL PARKS AND DESERTS

Sequoia National Park, Kings Canyon National Park, Yosemite National Park, Lassen Volcanic National Park, Crater Lake National Park, Mount Ranier National Park, North Cascades National Park, Mojave Desert, Pumice National Desert.

***

EQUIPMENT CARRIED

One man tunnel tent, Fairydown Dragonfly - Excellent.

Backpack, Macpac 'Cascade' 90litre + pack cover - Excellent.

Asolo Boots - very strong and comfortable.

Sleeping Bag, Fairydown Liteweight Entrant - too light, heavier down fill would have been better.

Ice axe - Indispensable.

Crampons - Made life comfortable at times, but could have got by with just the ice axe.

Gaiters - Good for snow and tick protection.

Ground pad, Therma-Rest - very comfortable.

Polypropylene clothing - 1 T shirt, 2 long sleeve crew necks, 1 Long Johns. (polyprop is excellent - light, quick drying, warm when wet.)

Hiking shorts.

Track suit trousers - Good for cold weather and camp wear.

Waterproof Overtrousers, Gortex - Excellent.

Fleece, Fairydown Polar Plus - Excellent.

Anorak, Gortex - Excellent.

Balaclava - polypropylene, Woollen Watch cap, Brimmed hat - canvas.

Bandanna, for neck sun protection.

Gloves, Woollen mittens double thickness.

Gloves, polypropylene finger - For wear under the mittens.

Cotton T shirt - waste of time, cold when wet, should have been another polyprop.

Cotton shirt. Socks - 3 pairs Woollen, 3 pairs polyprop inners.

Underpants, 2 pairs - One pair for California and a change at the Oregon Border!!

Jandals (Flip Flops/thongs) - Good light camp footwear to air the feet.

Stove, MSR International - Excellent, but be sure to carry field maintenance kit.

2 Fuel bottles, Stove maintenance kit.

Pot with lid, 1 spoon, 1 plastic mug.

Water bottles - 4x two litre plastic soft drink bottles. (These are indestructible, light, flatten when empty and cheap.)

Swiss Army knife - with scissors for trimming toenails!

Compass with variation setting adjustment (less mental arithmetic when you're tired)

Map and trail guide - "Pacific Crest Trail" by Wilderness Press, Excellent, indispensable.

First Aid kit (Usual, plus painkiller/anti inflammatory drug)

Snake Bite kit, nylon stuff bag for bear bagging, Several plastic trash bags, Sun Lotion, Insect repellent, Lip balm, Toothbrush, Paste, Toilet paper, Spare laces, Sewing kit, Tent patch kit, Velcro tape, Superglue, String, Lighters, Waterproof matches, Mightylite torch, Spare batteries, Sunglasses (Blinker type and conventional), Thermometer, Walkman radio, Iodine tablets, Water filter.

Parachute chord 50 metres.

Pedometer (This broke during a fall on one of the passes, but had served it's purpose, as by then I could accurately assess mileage by time and terrain)

Camera, film, notebook, pen, pencil.

Hooks, line, bait.

FOOD and WATER!

***

Cascade Range, Washington

And finally, here's a cheerful little quote from John Muir...

You may be a little cold some nights, on mountain tops above the timber-line, but you will see the stars, and by and by you can sleep enough in your town bed, or at least in your grave.

Heading for a pass

***

Made in the USA
Middletown, DE
16 November 2015